# TEMPEST, FLUTE, & OZ

## ALSO BY FREDERICK TURNER

**NONFICTION**

*Shakespeare and the Nature of Time*
*Natural Classicism: Essays on Literature and Science*
*Rebirth of Value:*
*Meditations on Beauty, Ecology, Religion, and Education*

**FICTION**

*A Double Shadow*

**POETRY**

*Between Two Lives*
*Counter-Terra*
*The New World*
*The Garden*
*Genesis*

# TEMPEST, FLUTE, & OZ
## Essays on the Future

## Frederick Turner

PERSEA BOOKS NEW YORK

*For information, write to the publishers:*
*Persea Books*
*60 Madison Avenue*
*New York, New York 10010*

**Library of Congress Cataloging-in-Publication Data**
*Turner, Frederick, 1943–*
*Tempest, flute, and Oz: essays on the future / Frederick Turner.*
*p. cm.*
*Includes bibliographical references.*
*ISBN 0-89255-159-3 : $19.95*
*1. Twenty-first century—Forecasts. I. Title.*
*CB161.T84 1991*
*303.49′09′05—dc20*

*Designed by REM Studio, Inc.*
*Set in 10/13 Century Schoolbook by ComCom, Allentown, Pennsylvania.*
*Printed and bound by Haddon Craftsmen, Scranton, Pennsylvania.*
*First Edition*

*For Mei Lin*

# CONTENTS

# ACKNOWLEDGMENTS

A BOOK OF THIS SORT IS REALLY A record of a set of conversations; I hope the record can be even a fraction as interesting as the originals. I wish to thank the following for their wisdom and illumination: Alex Argyros, Robert Corrigan, David Channell, William Jordan, Bonnie Marranca, Lynda and Michael Sexson, Lewis Lapham, Jack Hitt, James Hans, Michael Benedikt, Daniel Turner, Edie Turner, Pat Howell, Thomas Fleming, Thomas Scheff, and Karen Braziller. I would also like to give special thanks to my students and other colleagues at the School of Arts and Humanities at the University of Texas at Dallas, and to the Fellows of the Dallas Institute of Humanities and Culture. There are too many others to list, but they know who they are.

An earlier and largely different version of "The Universal Solvent" was first published in *Performing Arts Journal* 34/ 35. "The Meaning of Value," in a slightly different version, first appeared in *New Literary History,* Vol. 21, No. 3, Spring 1990. In an abridged and differently organized form, "Life on Mars" first appeared in *Harper's,* August 1989. And "Angels from the Time to Come" was first published, in virtually the same form, in *Chronicles: A Magazine of American Culture,* April 1990. I wish to thank the editors of these periodicals for their help and encouragement.

# TEMPEST, FLUTE, & OZ

# INTRODUCTION

 WE STAND ON THE VERGE OF A NEW epoch of culture and history. Consider the successful revolutions in Eastern Europe and the Philippines, the recent movement toward democracy in South Africa, Namibia, Nicaragua, Brazil, Argentina, and other Latin American countries, and the temporarily unsuccessful attempts to overthrow totalitarianism in Burma and China. These revolutions are the signs of an emerging new cultural worldview, which is the subject of this book.

Not that these essays will pick up once again the old political themes, the weary and bloody struggle between left and right, that so dominated the thinking of the masses and their rulers during the period ironically named "modern," and that still dominates the thinking of many academic humanists. Indeed, those millions who risked their lives in demonstrations against their oppressors were in revolution against the whole political idea of left versus right.

They were rejecting the attempt to enforce a better way of life upon people than they would choose for themselves (that is, the best rationale for the one-party system). They were rejecting the idea that the media are tools of the rich and powerful to oppress the masses, and were showing that the use of the modern media—television, fax, etc.—tends to expose and weaken the oppressor, even when the oppressor apparently controls that use. They were rejecting the censorship of the arts for political correctness. They were rejecting the enforcement of any system of economic valuation not based on the free market of goods and ideas. They were rejecting the attempt by force to impose on people both social equality ("normalization" for the masses) and social inequality (the "leading role" for members of the Party). They were rejecting the brutal mistreatment of human nature and of nature in general by an economically-reductive but inefficient technology. And they were rejecting the idea that religion is a dying remnant of an obscurantist and oppressive past.

But though the fundamental propositions of the left have been trenchantly denied by the new movement, so too have many favorite ideas of the right. The scientific ideas that the new movement embodies—the evolving universe, the place of human beings within nature, the new knowledge of the brain and of human nature—are profoundly unsettling to traditional conservative views. Although those ideas overturn the socioeconomic determinism of the left, they are also fatal to the ethnocentrism, sexism, and racism of the far right. The naturalistic and evolutionary theologies that are emerging are likewise anathema to religious fundamentalists. The new technologies of transportation, communication, cybernetics, bioengineering, and biomedicine must undermine any conservative attempt to preserve social privilege, economic stasis, and hidebound nationalism. The new movement takes for granted many ideas, such as racial and sexual equality, that were originally the property of the left.

One of the fundamental characteristics of the new movement is its environmental conscience. Here again it rejects both the right and the left. For though left-wing theorists were quicker to jump on the bandwagon to attack environmental destruction than those of the right, left-wing regimes have arguably done more actual damage than right-wing ones. The labor theory of value, espoused alike by traditional right-wing economists and by the Marxist doctrine of the productive role of the proletariat, is being unraveled by new, delightful methods of production. The central priority of the new movement, world peace, is an explicit rejection of the myth of conflict that has dominated both right and left for so long. The left and the right have simply been left behind.

This book is an attempt to answer the question, "What next, then?" But it will not deal with immediate political consequences—its author not being qualified for such a task. Rather, it will seek to articulate the spirit of the new epoch, the epoch which will succeed modernism, and toward which postmodernism is an uneasy phase of transition.

As such it cannot be a scholarly book. Though its author can claim scholarship in various fields, it is essentially as a poet that he must try to express the mood and imagery and promise of the new millennium. Nor is this book a standard piece of futurology. Futurologists forget the past, and the past will be as much the past for the future as it is for us. In fact, many eras, like the Renaissance, have achieved their most brilliant originality through insight into, and an attempt to emulate, the glories of the past. While futurology usually addresses the outward conditions of future life, these essays focus on its heart and spirit. This collection claims no more than to be a myth. But it claims no less either.

The book begins with philosophical and theoretical explorations of the nature of our present puzzle. It then presents an explanatory myth for the future, and finally demonstrates some of the practical and experiential consequences of this new way of thinking.

The first essay surveys the powerful solvents that are dissolving the elements of culture throughout the world, so as to bring them into contact, and even into fusion, with one another. It begins with a discussion of interculturalism, but goes beyond this to briefly assess the current state of world economics and world culture. It focuses especially on a new phenomenon in the nature of production: it is going to be easier to make things than to discard them, and thus a new economics must emerge to accommodate this fact.

The second essay takes up the theme of value, and offers a new-old synthesis in which desire, economic value, truth value, ethical value, and aesthetic value can all be coherently accommodated. This synthesis is suggested and demanded by the new world that is being born; and it will involve a rebirth of the comic and tragic views of life (which were alike impossible under the regime of modernism).

The third essay proposes a central myth as a guide for our feeling and action in the next century. It develops and interprets the remarkable mythic story which can be found at the heart of three great and prophetic works of art: Shakespeare's *The Tempest,* Mozart's *The Magic Flute* (especially Ingmar Bergman's film version of it), and the 1939 MGM movie *The Wizard of Oz.* This mythic story is a renegotiation of the contract that the human race entered into in Eden, as it is told in countless human mythologies; and it is a story that we will need to take us on the next stage of our collective human journey.

The next two essays outline two proposals, growing out of that myth, for our work as a species in the next millennium. The first is the transformation of the planet Mars into a living ecology, a habitat for human and animal life. This work will give us, as a by-product, the knowledge we will need to save our own planet, and it will replace the old drives of war and conquest which have haunted us for so long. The second proposal is for the development of artificial intelligence, not as a narrow technical achievement (for as such, I argue, it will fail) but as a deep cultural and artistic project. As with the ancient art of alchemy, this work will result in a moral and spiritual transformation of ourselves, the alchemists.

The last essay is a jeu d'esprit, a playful speculation on the nature of angels. If we take the new physics seriously, we could argue that the angels are our descendants, and that they return and visit us, an inspiration to bring about the kind of world in which they can be born.

The synthesis that is called for in these essays has the effect of defusing other ideological conflicts than simply those between left and right. In the first essay, for instance, the merits of conflicting absolutist, relativist, and pluralist worldviews are debated, with the conclusion that, since none holds the last word, an evolutionary worldview which allows for the continuance of debate among them is preferable. In the second essay the struggle between the upholders and critics of the economic marketplace, of collective morality, of scientific truth, and of aesthetic values, which has erupted in fields as diverse as literary criticism, business ethics, sociobiology, and criminal justice, is shown to be based on a false assumption of the purity and unadulteratedness of value in itself; any individual value only exists when a hierarchy containing all types of value, however contested, is recognized. In the fourth essay the individual inadequacy of the reductive, the progressive, and the ecological ways of knowing the world is demonstrated, together with the need for synthesis of these often warring perspectives.

This book does not argue, however, for a cessation of disagreement and dialectical exploration. What it asserts is that many of the issues of modernity and postmodernity which are still the subject of bitter anger and conflict in the academy and in public policy are essentially dead and unproductive, and that much more promising areas of fertile and friendly argument are now opening up.

# THE UNIVERSAL SOLVENT: MEDITATIONS ON THE MARRIAGE OF WORLD CULTURES

 ANYONE WHO WALKS THE STREETS or campuses of the new tier of world-cities will be struck by the fantastic combinations of races in friendship, marriage, work, and study. My son, born in America, is half British and half Chinese; he plays baseball with a Slav from Poland and an Arab from Algeria; I eat at French/Lebanese, Thai, Salvadorean, and Israeli/Chinese restaurants, buy software from emigrant South Africans, celebrate the Zoroastrian New Year with Farsi friends from Iran, and collaborate on artistic and intellectual projects with a Macedonian Yugoslav, a Greek, a Hungarian Jew, a Japanese, a Latin American, and several Germans. Yet in a strange way the place I live in does not cease at all to be Texas to the core. Cultural information not only has the

property of being transferable without loss, but also of being almost infinitely superimposable. Many cultures can occupy the same place or brain without loss; there seems to be no cultural equivalent of the Pauli Exclusion Principle, which forbids two particles from existing in the same energy state and place at the same time.

What is the meaning of this unparalleled mixing that has been going on in recent years among the world's cultures? Interculturalism itself comes in a bewildering variety of genres, each with its own pressing and highly ambiguous set of moral and epistemological questions. Consider this brief and incomplete list of intercultural genres: tourism, international charity, evangelism, colonial administration, anthropology, true trade (as opposed to mercantile colonialism), political and military contacts, academic consultation and exchange, artistic collaboration, artistic influence, political asylum, statelessness, refugeeism, education abroad, intermarriage, and emigration.

Of course any celebration of a new era of tolerance and ethnic harmony would be premature. The collapse in our century of the great empires—the Austrian, the Turkish, the British, the Soviet, and soon the Chinese—has left large areas of the world in a state of Balkanized tribalism and nationalist hostility, and it well may appear that we are further away than ever from the interculturalism we anticipate. It may even seem a decadent luxury to trouble our conscience with the problems of cultural mixing when such a foul-tempered resurgence of racism and ethnocentrism is under way.

But from another perspective these horrible events are belated but inevitable consequences of world forces that will eventually lead to a more comfortably intercultural world. The great empires held those tensions in an artificial stasis, and now they are playing themselves out naturally. In this view the eventual result of the enormous mobility of persons and information will be something like the condition of the United States or the European Common Market; or like those countries which, having once possessed colonial empires, now have had their homelands peacefully invaded by their erstwhile subjects and find that together with the inevitable stress, there is also a surge of cultural revitalization that is not unwelcome.

Perhaps the most remarkable fact of the modern world is that for the first time—in just the last two decades—all the member cultures of the human race have finally come to know of each other, and have, more or less, met. There really is no human Other now. Clearly, the ethnocentrism of the old right and of political conservatism in general cannot survive the enormous influx of information from the rest of the world. Of course, our urge to demonize the Other has not gone away, whether the other is black or white, female or male, left-wing or right-wing; it has even sometimes been artificially displaced to other species and even to some of our more human-like machines. But the urge must now contend with the logic of history, technology, and economics.

The formal complexity of interculturalism has not prevented some of our bolder, and paradoxically, more conventional, intellectuals from seeking to cut the gordian knot of the problem with the sword of neoleftist analysis. A very crude reduction of their position might go like this: the rich are bad, and the poor are good. The rich got rich by exploiting the poor, and then by rigging the cultural value system to justify their privileges. The same goes for nations as well as for individuals. Nowadays, the old form of international expropriation, colonialism, has been partly replaced by a new form, whereby the bad (rich, powerful, white, male, etc.) expropriate the cultural property of the good (poor, weak, etc.). This theory attacks anthropologists, collectors of tribal art, tourists, Western followers of Oriental religions, white jazz enthusiasts, performance artists who use foreign traditional artistic and ritual techniques, and even male collectors of quilts and women's arts, as expropriators of the cultural goods of others. Recently, the singer David Byrne was attacked by *Rolling Stone* magazine for "ripping off" Hispanic music in his new album. Critics of contemporary culture are thus claiming that cultural exchange is a form of economic exploitation.

But at least implicitly the left now recognizes culture as having real economic value of its own, rather than simply being a smokescreen to conceal the true, economic, facts of coercion, power, and control; for otherwise the parallel between economic exploitation and cultural appropriation would have no meaning. If culture is a kind of goods that can be stolen by the powerful, then it is a goods.

Some kind of plausibility might be constructed for the economic/cultural exploitation argument. But a few further examples serve to show how flimsy it is. Consider Japan's success in exporting its products, including much of its material and spiritual culture, to the United States. The expropriation model, to be consistent, would imply that the United States was expropriating the cultural property of Japan. More absurd still, the enormous penetration of American music, movies, television, soft drinks, sports activities, and consumer goods into many of the poorer Asian, African, and Latin American countries would have to be interpreted as the expropriation on a huge scale of American cultural property by Third World cultural colonists.

Ah, but that's different, the determined neo-Leninist might say. But how is it different? Every answer leads to greater and greater betrayals of socialist articles of faith, some of them shared by all people of good will. Is it that the poor benighted natives (or poor benighted Americans) are in an unequal cultural contest and ought to be protected for their own good from our (or Japan's) potent and corrupting forms of cultural firewater? Besides being rather condescending, this arguemnt is virtually identical to that of the supporters of apartheid in South Africa. Or is it that the

terms of the exchange are unfair—that the Third World does
not get a fair price for its cultural goods, while we gouge
them for ours? This argument assumes either that there is
some ultimate authority that decides which cultural goods
are more valuable, ours or theirs, and does not trust either
our valuation of relative value or theirs; or that there might
be such a thing as a *fair* trade (and thus the possibility of a
free market, entrepreneurism, and the whole capitalist ensemble). And if we use the Japan-U.S. example, it is the
cheapness, not the dearness, of Japanese goods that is the
problem. When it comes down to it, the only difference between being culturally expropriated and conducting cultural imperialism is who we thought in the first place were
the good guys and the bad guys.

The whole argument is based on a misleading analogy
between cultural goods and industrial goods; which in turn
is based on ignorance of the difference between information
and matter. If matter is transferred to another location it
ceases to exist at its first location. Moreover, it takes work
to make the transfer, and if that work is paid for out of the
matter that is being transferred, one ends up with less matter at the point of arrival than at the point of origin. A
steamship gets to its destination lighter than when it left its
home port. However, if information is transferred, it not
only remains where it started, but it is not necessarily diminished by its travels. The sender of information by radio does
not cease to know what she knew when she sent it off in the
message; and the message can be made redundant enough to
include an arbitrarily diminishing amount of error.

In the mysterious realm of physics which deals with the
thermodynamics of information, the energy cost to a compu-
tational system—that is, a system which does work by creating and/or transferring information—is in theory incurred
only when it comes time to destroy the excess information
that has built up in the system. Thus, one could in theory
design a process for mass-producing pieces of information,

whose only expense would be erasing the tape afterwards. If information is a kind of goods, then it is one which costs the maker nothing to make but which obliges its consumer to find an expensive waste-disposal system for the purchase once it is used. The logic and justice of such a transaction are almost unknown to contemporary economics, and the laws of intellectual property lag woefully behind the astonishing expansion of information-space that is now taking place in the world.

Yet do we not recognize in these goods, which it costs virtually nothing to buy but which clutter up the house and alarm environmentalists when we try to dispose of them, an increasing proportion of our own property? And if we are cultural workers, do we not recognize—though unwillingly, because it concedes how much fun our work is—those goods we create but cost us nothing to do so? And is not cultural property much more the kind that costs nothing to make or buy, that does not decay but is hard to get rid of, than the old kind, dear to Marxists and Capitalists alike, that costs the groaning labor of workers to produce, which they lose by giving to us and must be compensated for, and which wears out only too swiftly as we consume it?

It is the "expropriators" of cultural goods, then, not their creators, who are exploited. And thus the expropriation explanation collapses in absurdity.

But this meditation has already generated issues—or created information!—which it would be interesting to pursue. For instance, if it costs cultural creators nothing to produce their goods, why should they be paid? This question is not as trivial as it might appear; for as automation performs more and more repetitive and mechanical work that used to be done by humans, all workers will approach the economic condition of artists. And a theory that bases value on labor will be totally inadequate. An artist, for instance, may labor very hard at versification, draughtsmanship, secretarial detail, athletic training, or musical technique; but what we value most highly in the productions of artists is precisely that which transforms their labor into an addictive joy, which they would seek out whether they were paid or not. We do not pay artists for their *labor:* a bad artist may labor more tenaciously than a good one, but produce worthless results, as Peter Schaffer eloquently demonstrated in his play *Amadeus.* Yet if they were not paid, we would not have cultural producers, which would be a pity; even artists have to eat. Somehow there must be a medium and a method of exchange between cultural goods and the material goods which, as we say, keep body and soul together.

Another problem: If it is the audience for cultural goods that is doing the work—erasing the tape—then shouldn't they, too, be paid? Do we not already pay them, in fact, by subsidizing out of the public purse the cost of using the library, the museum, the symphony, the university, the theater? The poorest persons in our society have cheap access to a large part of the cultural riches of the world—certainly to a larger part of it than would an ancient emperor or Renaissance duke. And if we pay both cultural producers and cultural consumers, who foots the bill? Can money itself, in such an economy, "grow on trees" the way information clearly can? But can we retain our traditional respect for artists and other cultural producers if we pay them *despite* the fact that, as artists (rather than draughtsmen, clerks, or athletes) they do no work; and that we pay audiences to go and see them, *and to selectively forget what they have seen and heard?* Can we replace the matter-based, or industrially-based, model of respect with another more suited to the new age that is coming? Obviously, artists do indeed do something like what we used to call work, and their audience receives the most valuable goods of all; but the many jokes and tragic stories about working parents who do not want their children to grow up to be layabout artists also have a grain of truth.

These economic paradoxes are not problems only for the cultural and information economies. Indeed matter cannot be transferred without cost; but to what extent are we actually buying matter even when we buy a thing as solid as a car or a washing machine? In fact, increasingly, we're buying a very complicated and effective piece of information. The matter doesn't matter: some of the steel in my car was actually once a washing machine, and before that, another car. When my car no longer holds its information, I may pay someone to tow it away. What form—what information—the factory put into the matter is what counts. I wouldn't want or pay for a lump of steel; what I buy is the information the factory put into the steel, information increasingly transferred by robot machines without human labor. Steel itself is a kind of information imposed by atomic and crystalline structure upon neutrons, protons, and electrons. Traditional economics still depends on the need for information to be embodied in, and thus tagged by, the matter of its incarnation; just as traditional copyright law still depends on the physical means of publication. The debate in Congress which took place in 1989 over the importation from Japan of cheap high-quality digital tape recording machines shows that we have almost reached the limits of the old kind of economics, and the old kind of thinking, altogether.

By "old" I do not mean here ancient and preindustrial, but rather pertaining to the conventional economic wisdom of modern societies. In fact we may have to resort to the thoughtways of traditional or folk societies, in combination with new imaginative constructs from the age of information, to be able to make sense of the new economics. Much of the riches of an ancient person was what she had in her head, as information; and as the new age develops, much of our riches will be in the form of totally intangible information contained in, but not confinable to, our cybernetic mental prostheses. As I write it, this essay becomes an immaterial process constituted by the interaction between my nervous system as I watch the screen of the word-processor, and a set of electromagnetic relations in its random access memory. But I still think of it as a text on paper, or at least as a picture of one. My son spurns the electric racing cars that I, as a boy, would have coveted, and prefers the meaningful pattern of electric charges embedded int the silicon of a computer video game. The computer game itself is not a picture of any thing that ever was, in the modern sense of "thing." In a sense, my son is a more tribal person than I am, even though I have had access through traditional humane learning to the ancient tribal sources of non-materialist economics—or should I say "oeconomics," in the traditional sense of housekeeping?

We may even, as we evolve towards an economics more like that of traditional societies than like that of our recent modern past, come to a wiser appreciation of their ethics and aesthetics. For such societies, true riches are within; nobody can copyright a great poem because everybody knows it by heart; the chief value that society possesses is the information—the skills of beauty, weaving, prophecy, storytelling—embodied in the limbs and nervous systems of its Helens, its Cassandras, and its Penelopes.

Already the West is getting tired of mere consumer goods, of commodities. On our urban beltways we can now find business establishments that rent storage space so that we can get rid of our possessions without ceasing to possess them. Possession is becoming very abstract. Our best possessions are empty space and time. We are becoming a "service economy" rather than a manufacturing economy. Ironically, it is often those critics of American society—liberal economists and socialist political philosophers—who are most critical of our materialism, that are also most vocal in deploring the decay of our factories and the movement toward those intangible forms of economic activity we label "services."

But perhaps their complaints are inconsistent. Are we not becoming at last literally less materialistic? Should we not prefer service to things? The Japanese themselves, the heroes of manufacturing, are now rushing to export their manufacturing function to the little dragons of the Pacific rim; the socialist bloc has gone broke trying to hang on to a manufacturing economy. Having persuaded the rest of the world to become harried producers and consumers of material goods, we may in a generation or two have so transformed ourselves by our information technology that we will have become the wise old sages, like Yoda in *Star Wars,* counseling brash, driven, young Asians on the mysterious ways of spiritual enlightenment and the traditional wisdom of the body electric. Already artists like Seichi Ozawa and Akira Kurosawa are finding the West more hospitable than their bottom-line oriented homeland to their artistic and spiritual visions.

We would seem to be approaching a time when cultural goods are going to be the only kind there are, and material—matter itself—will have dissolved into a brilliant and pliable haze of interpenetrating probability-domains. New forms of manufacturing, such as nanotechnology and biotechnology, are on the horizon, that will radically transform our conception of matter. The requirements and luxuries of physical existence, according to the prophets of the new technologies, will be supplied by self-reproducing, self-programming, and independently-foraging Von Neumann machines, nanotechnological miniature factories invisible to the naked eye. Those unseen agencies will be much like what ancient cultures and classical civilizations called spirits, genii loci, kamis, naiads, dryads, angels, nymphs, dakkinis, demons, gremlins. Nature is already full of such entities: the bacteria which ferment our cheeses, the DNA of plants and animals—but they are the results of evolution unassisted by conscious awareness. We ourselves, most potent of wood-

demons, came about when our own consciousness, expressed
and mediated by our kinship rules and mating rituals, took
a hand in evolution. Now we have begun to extend that
conscious hand to the evolution of the rest of nature.

What kind of world economy will come out of the
changes I am describing? Perhaps the closest analogy might
be the Homeric economy, the world of gift-giving, hospital-
ity, the ritualization of obligation, sacrifice, deed as performance, and bardic commemoration of deeds that we find in the
*Odyssey* and the *Iliad*. Such an economy is the only kind
that makes sense when matter is no longer a reliable numerical index of value. That ancient world was one explicitly
conceived as densely populated with intention, spirits, local
deities, and so on. The value of a sword or shield was the
weight of story, of software, that it bore—the density of information, of spirit, embodied in Achilles' sevenfold shield is
both what makes it a good shield and what identifies it as of
divine make. Odysseus' story, the tale he brings back from
the sack of Troy, is worth to the Phaeaceans a shipload of
treasure; and those treasures themselves are worth only the
stories stamped and embedded in them. Homer's own living
is his tale.

But there is no copy-protection on this story-informa-
tion. Thus no system of contracts, patent and copyright laws,
bills of sale, and specie-backed currency, can ensure an orderly and just disposal of such goods if they are conceived of
as material commodities. The only thing that cannot be copied in Homer's story is the power and immediacy of his own
performance of it, his personal presence, that which cannot
be measured as a commodity—his gift, as we say.

Homer's world is an economy of sacrifices, performance,
and gifts; the greatest profit consists in the greatest sacrifice,
the act or deed is not just the legal sign but the reality, the
limits of this economy are not how *much* one is prepared to
give in exchange for what one wants, but how *little*. It is the
predatory givers of that world, the masters of the potlatch

and the holocaust (in the old sense) that are the greatest dangers, not, as in the world of mercantile colonialism and early capitalism, the predatory takers. To take Troy, Agamemnon must first have given his own daughter Iphigenia. Beware of the Greeks when they come bearing gifts, especially Trojan Horses. According to an ancient etymology the gift (in English) may also be poison, "das Gift" (in German); the rhinegold is the kiss of death. Life is the performance, and thus the death, of the hero.

Where the analogy between the future and Homer's universe breaks down is of course in those aspects of ancient Greece that really have been set behind us by the ratchet of historical memory. It was a martial universe, one in which a violent rabble of young male heroes confronted a violent and uneasy patriarchy, contending over, and divided radically from, that third mysterious indoors world of the matriarchy, of white arms and weaving and procreativeness and terrifying protected personal subtlety. Since that time Christ has come, we have learned to love our neighbor (and to send to the gas-chambers those who do not subscribe to the rationale of that love!), and to extend the idea of equality to all human creatures, male and female (except our children!). The point of the analogy is that a hard, real-feeling, complex world does exist in Homer *in which nobody buys anything from, or sells anything to, anyone else.* As such it is an imaginable human world based on gifts, on performance, on the exchange of informational goods. And such a world may now be approaching.

Already in our own time it is the entertainers—the pop-singers, film stars, sports heroes who create cultural information—that are the highest-status members of society, and often the richest. One year Paul McCartney was the richest person in England after the Queen. Ancient princes might well be described as the great public entertainers of their times, the sacrificial superstars whose exploits formed the basis of the stories that gave meaning to life. Agamemnon steps upon the magic carpet woven by Queen Clytemnestra, and his blood nourishes a cycle of stories—concentrated information—that define the wealth of the archaic Greek economy. John Lennon dies for our sins. We elect an actor for our king and watch while he is resurrected from the wound of the assassin's bullet; and so according to the logic of mythology, a dead king is reborn and the pollution of his death in Dallas is purified.

How might the Homeric/cybernetic economy work *between* cultures, rather than within one? In Homer, if the hero comes across a tribe that is sufficiently barbarous as to be no part of the Greek world, the only possible relation he can have with it is as its food or indeed as its proto-colonialist expropriator: consider Odysseus' encounters with the Laestrygonians and the Cyclopes. For us, the whole world is as a Hellenized Mediterranean. What universal solvents will ensure the liquidity and translatability of cultural value? What new problems and dangers will be spawned by our very success? How do we preserve the cultural differences that we value?

The first of these questions, about universal solvents, requires some explanation. The human mind, and human culture in general, has admirable powers of compartmentalization. As any teacher knows who has experienced the coexistence in a student' mind of contradictory information (for instance, astronomical, biological, and geological book-learning together with a belief in the literal Biblical account of creation), "cut and dried" knowledge can leave the mind virtually unscathed. Contradictions do not even consciously arise; such knowledge has its own cocoon of insulation. To change the metaphor, the mixing of colors, or the metabolism of a ferment, or chemical reactions, or cookery, cannot take place without a liquid medium that presents the dissolved or suspended elements intimately and extensively against one another. Dry paints cannot mix.

The ready availability of multicultural information is not enough in itself to initiate the mysterious alchemy of interculturalism, whether that alchemy is the change in an individual's value system, or a transformation in the economic system and its underpinning of copyright law. All past bigotries and ethnocentrisms have coexisted with some, even much, information about other cultures. What is needed, and what our age has supplied, is a group of solvents that can serve as a common medium for all kinds of cultural information and insure that whatever processes of transformation they can engender in each other will actually happen. What are those solvents?

Most obvious, perhaps, is the instantaneous medium provided by worldwide telecommunications, especially television. There is a peculiar difference between radio and television in this respect, which has been ignored by the critics of television. Curiously enough, it was the age of radio which saw the last great spasmodic surge in nationalism, ethnocentrism, dictatorship, and mass ideology. It was radio that broadcast the mystagogic rant of Hitler, the brutal rhetoric of Stalin, the tirades of Franco and Mussolini. In a sense, the Allied Powers in the Second World War were lucky in getting as leaders Roosevelt, Churchill, and de Gaulle, who had a patrician loyalty to democracy, because the power that radio and its associated technologies provided them might well have been a temptation to dictatorship.

Even though television, like radio, is a broadcast medium, and thus would seem to favor the domination of a passive mass audience by a great authoritative voice, the nature of the visual medium subtly undermines the power and impressiveness of those who would use it. Somehow, if we can see the man live, see the play of expression on his face, his mortal human body taking up space in the world, turning its back, stumbling on the helicopter steps like Gerald Ford's, or dropping the banquet morsel from its chopsticks as Deng Xiaoping's did recently on television, then we cannot take his speeches very seriously. Part of it is that we can see how old he is. If he is old, we see the signs of decrepitude; if young, we feel superior to the fellow. I use the masculine pronoun here because, very significantly, female leaders do not seem to be afflicted by the television feet of clay. The great warlords of the recent past have often been women: Golda Meir, Indira Gandhi, Chiang Ching, Margaret Thatcher. In the film medium, as Leni Riefenstahl knew, the visual awkwardness can be more or less edited out, but live television is fatal to a demagogue. The only U.S. president to use television well was, significantly, a film actor. Knowing the medium, Ronald Reagan could use its deficiencies for his own purposes, and gain sympathy by playing subtly against his own mortal infirmities. His enemies did not realize this, and the more they attacked his apparent deafness, inattention, and wandering memory, the more affection he got. But it was affection, not obeisance.

Television is a humanizing medium, and a leveler. It also transcends, as radio does not, the barriers of language. That was why the students in Tienanmen square put up their statue to Democracy: as a visual symbol that would speak across the variety of languages both in the world at large and in China itself, where dozens of different languages are spoken. The man who stopped the tanks was making an utterance that is universally human. Television is thus a solvent for all cultural differences.

In the long run, other telecommunication media may be even more potent as solvents. Though the telephone is language-bound, it is not a broadcast medium, and thus, while enabling diverse populations within a language community to exchange ideas, cannot be used for domination of populations. Wiretapping is not a commensurate compensation for the authorities, as the Polish government tacitly admitted eight years ago when, after declaring martial law and outlawing Solidarity, it closed down the telephone exchanges, thus foregoing the potentially valuable intelligence it might have got by listening in. The facsimile or fax machine, as the Chinese students found, is becoming another strong solvent, especially when there is a language problem. Here a picture is worth a million words. Computer logic and computer languages have begun to erode the acoustic language barrier, and perhaps eventually artificial intelligence may make possible the cybernetic translation of natural languages. In any case, the growth of telecommunications has tended to reinforce the development of the English language itself as a lingua franca and thus as a universal solvent. The expansion of English by the addition of hundreds of thousands of international scientific and technical words (themselves based on the old lingua francas of Latin and Greek) is part of this trend. We will deal later with the explosion of devices for recording and playing music, and the effect this has had on cultural liquidity.

Related to the cultural solvent of telecommunications, and technically based on it, has been the emergence of international financial markets, and the multinational corporations. Through new kinds of financial and investment instruments, ownership by union and pension funds of foreign securities, and the worldwide accessibility of government bonds issued by many nations, large numbers of ordinary people now own substantial property in other countries. In fact there already exists a loose and tacit world currency composed of a combination of the old petrodollars, the U.S. budget deficit, and Third World debt. The world as a whole has discovered what Britain and America found in the late eighteenth century: the virtues of debt as a means of capital formation, its tendency to liquefy fixed assets and to put to work unused capital tied up in the real property of nations and, more intangibly, in the talents and education of their peoples and even in the probable political stability of their future.

Out of this world liquidity of value has come new institutions, especially the multinational corporations. These entities constitute the first examples of the true world citizen. This is not to say that they are especially virtuous; but for them there is no escape, the world itself being their field of action. They cannot emigrate, and thus their loyalty must be to the world as a whole. The welfare of a citizen of a nation is partly bound up with the welfare of that nation, and thus that citizen's vote will be motivated partly toward the national benefit, a motivation that mitigates his or her special interests. When citizens of the world are numerous and powerful enough, there will emerge a political quality akin to patriotism, an identification of one's own interests with those of the whole globe.

Another universal solvent is the global ecological crisis and the increasing awareness that it cannot be resolved by purely national means. Such threats as nuclear accidents like the one at Chernobyl, acid rain, the depletion of the ozone layer, species extinctions, and the greenhouse effect (with the accompaniment of global warming or a new ice age, depending on whose theories you accept) are world problems and require the liquefaction of different legal, industrial, and agricultural traditions in order to produce cooperative action. Related to this perceived crisis is the global danger of nuclear war and nuclear winter (or nuclear summer, according to some theorists). It is perhaps a blessing in disguise that the feedback mechanisms by which such changes might actually change the environment are as yet poorly understood. Even if alarm is misdirected, it is at least shared.

One of the most creative and positive solvents in world culture is the almost universal acceptance among the world's elites of the emerging scientific account of the universe. Here, though, there are dismaying counterforces: on both the right and the left there has been a backlash against the challenge and the cognitive expansion demanded by new developments in science. Evolution, for instance, is under attack by religious fundamentalists on one side, and by left-wing social determinists on the other, both anxious to avoid the responsibilities of creative and moral action demanded by the relationship between human nature and nature in general. The relaxation of social discipline brought about by cultural pluralism has itself been partly responsible for the new anti-science atmosphere. The hard disciplines of logic and mathematics, and the self-restraint and self-criticism required by scientific method, are now out of reach of many who, in a stricter academic climate, might have acquired the rudiments of them and so been liberated.

Nevertheless, science will surely win the race between enlightenment and reaction, because those societies and groups within society which have mastered science will generally be more effective, inventive, and moral than those which have not, and will thus have greater powers of cultural survival. "More moral," by the way, because more capable of self-examination.

The last, and in some ways the most intriguing, of the great solvents is the rhythm of contemporary popular music, specifically "rock music." Originating in a fertile combination of the sophisticated African musical tradition with European and Latin American elements, a new musical medium emerged in the Sixties which is perhaps the most potent, because the most fundamental, of all forces for change. For many years jazz and blues coexisted with classical and folk music; but gradually a mutual translation took place. The names of Scott Joplin, the Gershwins, Leonard Bernstein, Bob Dylan, the Beatles, and now David Byrne and Philip Glass, chart the process of development. One recalls moments of musical insight in it: "West Side Story," Procul Harum's "A Whiter Shade of Pale," which was simultaneously real Bach and the most psychedelic pop, George Harrison's adaptations of Indian sitar music, Paul Simon's work with South Africa's Ladysmith Black Mombaso, Glass's "Satyagraha" and "Koyannisqaatsi."

Essentially what happened was that a very simple, pan-human rhythmic beat was discovered, of no musical merit in itself, to which the music of all world cultures could be set and which served as a liquid medium that would enable musical syncretism to take place. What has followed has been a worldwide musical revolution, where a record made in London by a talented Indian singer using a reggae base and Brazilian arrangements will influence young Nigerian, Czech, and Japanese rock groups, and perhaps form part of the raw material for a new classical opera. The extraordinary phenomena of glasnost and democracy in Eastern Europe and the Far East may have as much to do with the universality of rock and roll music as with anything else. This is not a praise of rock in itself, which is a rather insipid form of sound; but rock has been like alcohol, which can serve as the base for the most exquisite blends of perfume, the most delicate liqueurs.

The world of Homer and his Odysseus is one united by a liquid medium, literally that universal solvent that we call the ocean, that Homer called the *polyphloisboiou thalasses,* the multitudinously-flowing sea. The ambivalent and two-faced god of that medium, Poseidon, is the key problem of the *Odyssey.* The poem is about oars, about how to use the destructive element, as Stein calls it in *Lord Jim,* to do creative work and to get home with the story of Troy. The trouble with a universal solvent is what to use as a containment vessel. If the solvent is truly universal, it will melt through any walls which try to hold it in. The solution to this riddle is the solution to the problems of our times. It is, essentially, the one barrier which stands in the way of those scientists attempting to achieve nuclear fusion, and thus a cheap, inexhaustible, and clean source of energy for all humankind. In physics, the universal solvent is a plasma. What bottle can contain this genie? Uncontained, it is the principle of the greatest threat to humanity, the hydrogen bomb. Contained, it is the potential hearth of us all.

Interestingly enough, the best solutions suggested so far for the containment of this Thunderer, this Poseidonic universal solvent, is to use it as its own container, either by allowing it to power and to control an electromagnetic field that will constrain it, or by using it as an inertial jet-propulsion force to collapse it into a state of such great density that it begins to produce more energy than it consumes. If we accept this answer to the riddle as having mythic force for the containment of the intercultural plasma, we must look for ways in which interculturalism will be self-controlling, or can be induced to enter turbulent but stable feedback states that maintain themselves. But first we must look more carefully at the dangers and diseases of the new informational economy that is emerging.

What are the main problems of interculturalism? One is immediately obvious: the issue of authenticity. It arises most clearly, perhaps, in the experience of tourism for both the tourist and the local population which serves and is photographed by the tourist. More subtly, but more disturbingly to the intellectual and artist, are such questions as: How authentic is my claim as an anthropologist to speak for the autochthones? Can I justify my ethnodramatic performance of their rituals? This haiku or Noh play I have written, or in which I am performing—is it genuine? Is my Buddhism authentic? Or again, how am I to feel about the modern factories on the outskirts of Athens, or the Kentucky Fried Chicken on Tienanmen Square? Or Japanese baseball and squaredancing? Or Zimbabwean rock and roll? Or my Vietnamese student's appreciation of the novels of Jane Austen?

The problem is fundamentally connected to the characteristic reproducibility of cultural (informational) goods: the fact that, unlike material objects, they are not destroyed at the point of origin when they are transferred to another place. When our fundamental model of the nature of cultural goods is pieces of matter, there can only be one original of anything. In other words, we can only worry about authenticity if we are materialists. A materialist knows that if there are two copies of something, at least one of them must be a fake. (Similarly, if two things apparently occupy the same place, at least one of them must be an illusion.)

The same suspicion can be found among materialist lovers of nature. For them, a restored or artificial prairie can never be a real prairie. What they ignore is that all living things are by nature copies: reproduction is part of the definition of life. Nor does nature even bother to copy correctly. Evolution can only take place because the copies are incorrect, and thus there is variation in a species, upon which natural selection can work. According to a materialist definition of nature, all life is inauthentic!

But suppose one understood culture to be, like nature, in its very essence a process of not-quite-correct copying, of transfer, of sexual and asexual recombination, of merging, mixing, miscegenation, and the mutual appropriation of information? Those who are nostalgic for the certainty of being they imagine among *les tristes tropiques* propose models of authenticity that are essentially closed semantic systems, hermeneutic circles impenetrable to any stranger. What they fail to take into account is that such systems must be as impenetrable and closed to their own younger generation as to any anthropological outsider. To put it another way, culture must always reproduce itself by indoctrinating its children, who start off as strangers; and irreversible slippage will happen in the process. The indoctrinators will be compelled to develop a subversive meta-consciousness of their own cultural material if only in deploying, enumerating, and organizing it so as to teach it and leave nothing out. The human child, as we know from the rapid change in all living languages, delights in creative misreadings and playful inversions; and the human adolescent is hormonally programmed to question and subvert the wisdom of the elders.

In the strict, materialist definition of authenticity, then, there is no such thing as cultural authenticity; so we must, since authenticity is a valuable concept, look for definitions other than uniqueness, untransferability, cultural or natural indigenousness. Authenticity must be sought, where Jesus enjoined us to judge, by the fruits of something rather than its grounds. Authenticity is moral, artistic, and intellectual power; there is a lesser authenticity also in sheer economic effectiveness. Contain the plasma in the plasma; let the problem of authenticity become the authentic and central theme of the work.

How does this solution apply to the uncomfortable tourist? Here it is a matter of art. If the tourist is there for good, deep, complex reasons, and if the host country or city has a coherent aesthetic of what it means to entertain tourists, there need be no inauthenticity. The city of Stresa, on Lake Maggiore, has been entertaining tourists, mostly in the summer from sweltering Rome, for the past two thousand years and has got very good at it. It would be inauthentic for the town to do anything else. And although the reasons its pilgrims might give for their visit have changed, Delphi is no more inauthentic now than it was when Oedipus consulted the oracle there three thousand years ago.

How do we get from cultural ethnocentrism to true interculturalism? The first step in the process usually involves institutions of which many now disapprove: empire, religious evangelism, and colonialism. Curiously enough, in order to break out of the bounds of their cultural limitations most peoples have had to pass through one of two morally evil experiences—of being dominated by a foreign cultural hegemony, or of being the hegemonic dominator. India and England are good examples. It is hard to say which experience is the more damaging in the long run, but the damage is necessary. It is the trauma suffered by any structure when it first encounters its corrosive, Poseidonic solvent. Very occasionally this first step can be accomplished when a group of refugees or emigrants which shares a common alienation from its parent cultures is able to band together to form a union, as did the American settlers; but even here a common hegemonic culture, embodied in the Enlightenment reasoning of the Constitution, was required. In effect, the hegemonic culture must *be* the solvent, and the experience of one's own worldview as solvent is a profoundly unsettling one, manifested eventually in a kind of collective guilt, inertia, and anomie.

What follows the first stage, of hegemony, is what we might call naive relativism. Just like a child who discovers one exception to a rule, and who in a kind of cynical dudgeon dismisses the validity of all rules, so a culture at this stage, having found that its own rules are not universal, assumes a total cultural relativity of all rules. This phase actually comes from a generous impulse, itself the product of the colonial administrator's or anthropologist's need to develop an ethic of impartiality and self-criticism (or of an equally generous recognition by members of an oppressed colonial people that their oppressor's culture has its own sense and beauty). The effect is that the primary stance of the anthropologist, of respect for other cultures, becomes partly disseminated throughout the population.

Sometimes this stance is adopted strategically, for the worst of reasons: as an excuse for hedonism and a relaxation of the demands and duties of adult human life. Margaret Mead's Samoa and the photographs of the naked tribespeople in *National Geographic* became in this way justifications for the "playboy philosophy." The Huichol peyote cult served a similar function a few years later. Difference is interpreted as licence, as permission; the very strict moral and ritual rules of traditional societies are ignored. Another use for cultural relativism is in its guise as cultural determinism. If a person's success in life is the result of overriding cultural forces, usually perceived as oppressive, then those who perceive themselves as unsuccessful have the advantage of being able to claim that it was not their own efforts that were at fault, but society; and that society owes them, regardless of their personal character or contribution, a handsome restitution.

Though superficially attractive, relativism is not a coherent intellectual position. Either it is uniquely, absolutely, and exclusively true, and thus the shattering exception to its own rule that all truth is relative; or it is no more true than any other intellectual position, in which case the absolutism of, say, Hitler's Germany or Khomeini's Iran is just as intellectually acceptable as is relativism. Interestingly enough, it was on these grounds that Derrida was unable to condemn apartheid as roundly as his critics wished, and there were some intellectuals who found it difficult, for similar reasons, to condemn the Ayatollah's death sentence against Salman Rushdie.

Naive relativism is still a reigning ideology in the American academy, enshrined in what some have called "oppression studies" or "victimology." The general population, though, has to some extent moved on to a more mature perspective. One of the oddities of our time is how in many humanistic and social-science fields the academy has ceased to lead the national consciousness, and has begun to drag behind it; rather as the Anglican clergy moved from being in the forefront of consciousness in the seventeenth and eighteenth centuries (witness Donne, Herbert, Herrick, and Swift) to being the butt of literary jokes in the nineteenth and twentieth.

The more mature perspective—the third phase in the intellectual passage—is what we might call pluralism: the acceptance and recognition of cultural difference and a commitment to coexistence and to a worldview that is not unified but diverse and disseminated. If it is objected that the general population is not as sophisticated as this, we may point to the values embodied in the most popular and even vulgar TV shows—"Donahue," "All in the Family," "Perfect Strangers," "Night Court," and so on—in which pluralism and tolerance have become not just one of a number of important ethical norms, but the supreme, even the exclusive one. In such programs the ideal end result is always the uncritical acceptance of different lifestyles and of relative morality. This ideal of tolerance is indeed rather noble, and contrasts tellingly with the sometimes vicious exclusivism of academic factions, which one would suppose to be providing intellectual and moral leadership. The sheep, alas, are well in advance of the shepherds.

But pluralism itself has certain profound problems. One is that we are not neurally organized to perceive the world in a fundamentally pluralistic way. Even if, say, we were to prove to our satisfaction that the vision of the compound insect eye gave a more accurate picture of things than the single eye of a human being, there is not much one could do about it. In actual fact, of course, a large part of an insect's brain is devoted to integrating all of its different views into a single program of action; and in another sense we humans do indeed have compound eyes, made of millions of retinal neurons, but again integrated into a single worldview by the visual cortex. The universe itself has, by overwhelming selective pressure, evolved us as unifying and integrating animals. The strong inference is that a unifying perspective is, as much as anything can be said to be, more likely to be true than a pluralistic one: if it were not more accurate, we would not have survived.

Despite its claims, "pluralism" is itself, paradoxically, a unifying perspective, but a rather procrustean one. What it does is reduce all cultural differences to a sort of grid of equal cultural black boxes laid out over an infinite plane, boxes whose external form is safely measurable but whose contents are incommensurable and thus unknowable, and which are, as it were, the fundamental monads or quanta of reality. Geometrically it resembles the characteristic grid-design of the American city, or the relationship between departments in an American multiversity. Though pluralism forbids any attempt to perceive one cultural box as containing another, and thus revealing a comparable and measurable internal structure, it is itself a sort of gigantic box containing all other boxes as its subordinate material. Thus, like relativism, it contains a subtle hegemonic ambition of its own.

One way of describing what is the problem with pluralism is to say that if the universe is curved, even a simple sphere, no grid of equal rectilinear blocks can cover (or "tile") it without overlap. Specialization, and the definition of smaller and smaller cultural units, might be seen as the desperate resource of an intellectual culture trying to resolve exactly this problem. If the squares are small enough, perhaps the distortions of the world's curvature will somehow go away. Pluralism is like a sort of oil, a liquid medium that merely holds its contents in suspension, and does not allow them to transform each other chemically.

Mere pluralism requires no change in one's own or one's neighbor's perspective; indeed, it is threatened by change, especially by any attempt to understand and imagine, and thus incorporate, the contents of another cultural box. It so fears hierarchy—one possible result of such an incorporation—that it would prefer ignorance. Its tolerance of other worldviews could well be described as neglect or even as a kind of intellectual cowardice. At its worst one could describe it as an abdication or shirking of the great human enterprise of mutual knowledge, communication (literally, "making one together"), and mutual transformation.

The final stage in the intellectual passage into a new world is beginning to emerge, prompted by an instinctive discontent with the limits of mere pluralism. We might give it various names: syncretism, evolutionary epistemology, natural classicism, dramatistic ontology, the informational or Homeric/cybernetic economy.

Beneath all cultural differences certain fundamental human powers and capacities are emerging, that require cultural triggers to express themselves. These powers and capacities include language, the fundamental genres of the arts (musical tonality, the dramatic/performative ability, poetic meter, visual representation, dance, and so on), fundamental moral instincts, a religious/mystical ability, and the scientific rationality by which we learn to speak the other languages of nature. These powers and capacities are genetic endowments, created by evolution and embedded in our neural structure. Thus, true collaboration between cultures, and even a unifying syncretism of them, is possible on this shared biological basis. In this work ancient wisdom and traditional lore will join hands with the most sophisticated studies of genetics, paleoanthropology, cognitive science, cultural anthropology, ethology, sociobiology, the oral tradition, and performance theory. The word that describes our historical experience of the joining of old and new is Renaissance.

All cultures and all worldviews will be seen as competing or cooperating together in a single evolutionary drama, in a dynamic ecology of thought that is the continuation by swifter means of the universal process of evolution. The relationship between cultural worldviews will not be that between black boxes, but between characters in an ongoing drama, who can change each other, marry, and beget mutual offspring. It is not simply that this drama establishes the truth of things; it is the truth of things.

In other words, we can have faith that once the bonds that hold human ideas and cultures locked into a solid configuration are loosed by the powerful solvents of our time, the elements of culture, being basically human, will have the hooks and valencies to permit them to build up new, coherent systems not limited to one ethnic tradition. Moreover, the new systems can be very flexible and need not purchase survival by a paranoid vigilance and rigidity. The conflict and miscegenation between and within such systems as they emerge is not a horrifying defilement or pollution, but the normal and healthy operation of an evolutionary ecology of ideas. Information will become the basis of a gift exchange economy, the inexhaustible currency of a new order of economics. The hard, the tragic, and the inflexible will not disappear, but will be valued aesthetically and treasured for its contribution to the richness of the world. Nor will it be turned into a tyrannical fetish and a standard of conformity. As the human race recognizes itself more and more as a "we," it will paradoxically be more and more surprised by the otherness of what was once considered familiar. How strange, how exotic, how attractive our own culture is! Is not this the strangest and most interesting of worlds?

Eventually, perhaps, that greatest of all Others, Nature itself, will be recognized also as part of the "we." This is a mystical idea: it is prefigured in the lyre of Orpheus, that could make animals, trees, and rocks listen with delight, or the ring of Solomon, which gave him understanding of the languages of birds and beasts; the magic flute, the staff of Prospero, the double-helix caduceus or metatron of Hermes and Moses. We will, having learned to command Nature, find that it is sweeter to converse with it, and bury the staff certain fathoms in the earth; and that we are Nature, and Nature is ourselves.

# THE MEANING
# OF VALUE

WHAT MAKES SOMETHING VALU-
able? Where does value come from? What is
value? What is the relation between the
different kinds of value—numerical value,
truth value, cash value, moral value, aesthetic value?

Professional economists today are by and large content
to ignore the issue of the origins of value, and to treat it, the
way eighteenth- and nineteenth-century scientists treated
matter, as if it were given, irreducible, indestructible, and
without internal articulation. If pressed, most economists
would now define value as "marginal utility," which means,
roughly, the relative usefulness of an object. The value of a
car, according to this approach, might be expressed in terms
of a mathematical relationship involving the number of cars

a person already owns, and the number of bus or plane tickets the person might exchange for the car.

But what makes an object useful? It is surely not merely its efficiency in doing what it is designed to do, but also how desirable is the goal of its design. Useful for what? Is not desire—which can make something valuable—itself valuable, and a possession that can be justly reserved to its begetters or inventors? A brand name can be sold for millions of dollars; surely what is being sold is, to a large extent, the pure substance of desire. If Sears were to buy the Givenchy designer label, it would be buying the abstract value of Givenchy style.

John Hicks' big book *Value and Capital* does indeed struggle with the issue of why people desire what they desire, but concludes that value is essentially just what his colleagues assumed—a given, based on our biological needs and drives. But the enormous gap between our physical needs and the extraordinary things that people buy shows us that the natural drive theory is either plain wrong or so tautologous as to be useless. It is no good being morally upset by this gap; it is the way things are, and attests to the glorious idea that humankind does not live by bread alone.

Furthermore, desires change radically. The French historian Fernand Braudel traces the rise and fall of the desire for such commodities as spices, sugar, cocoa from the medieval to the early modern period—desire so fierce it could create and topple empires, and yet which, in a century or two, would fade into a mild acceptability. New desires and hence new values arise, conceived upon the sea foam by advertising or poetry. Much early advertising *was* poetry. Consider mountain landscapes before the Romantic period: they were trash landscapes, where the loser tribes were driven, and which travelers passed through in closed coaches so as not to be overcome by horror. And perhaps it was poets such as

William Wordsworth and Friedrich Schiller who taught us to desire such landscapes as beautiful.

The fact that commercial advertising creates desire scarcely needs illustration, but that it creates value is harder to swallow. Yet it must be so. Critics of society, such as René Girard, Jacques Lacan, and Louis Althusser, are often horrified by the way that desire, and thus value, can be artificially created by an economic system in which people learn what is desirable by imitating the desires of others; it was Rousseau who began this line of thought. But why should we be scandalized? Why should not value be a product of the imagination, fetishizing selected parts of the world? Why should not such products of the imagination be shared within society? And why should not the imagination be as natural a creative force as evolution itself?

The "bottom line," then, is the most fantastical, unstable, chimerical, and relativistic of all concepts. If sensible economic strategy worked, capitalism would fail. Instead, it is the wonderfully rational socialist systems that collapse, undone by inflation or its reflex, the black market, whose fundamental roots are as mysterious as desire itself. All true economics are voodoo economics.

Nor is it even the commercial advertisers who are the ultimate determiners of desire. By and large, commercial advertisers have few ideas of their own; instead they parasitize the original growth of past artistic genius, of popular culture, of the religious and ideological Zeitgeist as it works itself out through the conversations of the human species, for the imagery that will generate the new fashion. A margarine that tastes like butter is advertised by the Earth Mother figure angrily declaring that it's "not nice to fool Mother Nature." Upscale television ads imitate the visual style of Rembrandt, Mondrian, Antonioni, and use poetic techniques of meter, trope, and double-entendre invented by long-dead poets. So if you really believe in the bottom line, you should go straight to the poets, the shamans, the wizards, the weird weavers of desire.

Human desire is inherently self-contradictory. The intention of every desire is to eradicate itself: hunger desires to be filled, and thus to disappear; lust to be sated, and so vanish. On the other hand, desire has this peculiar feature: the satisfaction of a more concrete, immediate, and attainable desire results in the birth of a less concrete, immediate, and attainable one. If our thirst is quenched, we want food; when we have eaten, we would sleep; when we have slept, we want sex; when we have had sex, we want love; and when we have love, we want Truth, Beauty, God, if we know how to want them. Thus desire is, as it were, ratcheted so as to conduct us out of mere tropisms and appetites and into regions both higher and more problematic.

The thought that desire, and therefore value, might be created or generated *ex nihilo,* and that it might be the same token disappear, is abhorrent to the economists, because it introduces a wild card into that dismal science. Yet the fact that matter and energy can be created and destroyed was finally accepted by the physicists, who had even stronger reasons to fear it. What we need to look for, perhaps, is a sort of quantum theory of economics, which will open up our options for hypothesis, and then a sort of evolutionary economic theory which will show how we got from "there"—our ancestral primate community economics—to "here."

The search is not totally without signposts. I think we may find some of them in our language about value—that is, I think that one of the fields of observation and experiment where such a theory might be substantiated is the realm of language. The words we use to speak of such matters are fraught with pregnant ambiguity and multiple meanings. Take the word "goods." Goods, to be indeed goods—and not rubbish, for instance—must be good. "Good," though, is a term that is applied indiscriminately to moral actions, philosophical arguments, works of art, and valid checks. The word itself refuses to make the distinctions for us, and even seems to be trying to persuade us that they are all related. The same goes for "value," which can be aesthetic, logical or referential, moral, and financial. Or "bond," which can refer to a condition of captivity or slavery, to a freely entered and equal legal contract, to a financial instrument bearing a certain value, to an unhealthy emotional addiction, or to the tenderest, most loving, and most voluntary of all associations. "I love you according to my bond," says Cordelia to Lear. Take another word, "interest," which is intellectual curiosity, personal involvement, financial liability, and usury. Or "use," itself, with its great wobbling pyramid of meanings and connotations. Or "property"—a philosophical attribute defining the very self of an object or person in one sense (the French *propre* nicely catches the personal elements), but a "mere" possession in another; with a hint of what is proper, right, fitting, thrown in.

Perhaps the most fascinating word is "mean," which ranges in meaning from the lofty heights of "meaning" itself, through the "Golden Mean," the acme of perfect artistic proportion, the workmanlike "means" to an end, the bland but essential connector of the "mean" as average, and the plutocratic lever of financial "means," to the "meanness" of the miser and of what is most base and even cruel.

The wisest book that was ever written on this subject, Shakespeare's *Merchant of Venice,* puns relentlessly on all these multiple meanings. And when Shakespeare puns, we know that the language itself is shuddering and giggling, because its private parts, its organs of generation, are being touched and handled. So bewildering are the puns of that play that there seems to be a meaning beyond the meaning of any particular connection that is being made by similarity of sound or double-entendre or etymological derivation. That inner meaning is something like this: the meaning of meaning is to be found in the propensity of words to be mixed up with each other in the realm of their physical manifestation as sonic objects and as historical roots. This miscegenation, this incest, this promiscuous coupling of words, is fertile of meaning and value. It can be the means to a heavenly harmony; it is a loving risktaking whose tolerance and mercy is the same as those physical tolerances that make motion and happening possible in the world of matter—the liquidity of blood as opposed to the solidity of flesh; it is that generosity of being that droppeth like the gentle rain from heaven.

The puns of *The Merchant of Venice*, which connect words in such a way as to make them suggest higher meanings, are like those bonds of sexual attraction, desire, affection, love, and friendship by which we weave or fabricate such Heaven on Earth as may be. But this playing fast and loose with meanings, this agreement to relax the rules, this tolerance, this mercy, this generosity, cannot be divorced from a certain inherent corruption, injustice, complacency, unfairness, arbitrariness. Shylock, who wants justice and a one-to-one correspondence between word and meaning, is undone by the puns of the Christians. Perfect justice can exist only if a word can be divorced from the sound which makes it incarnate, actual in the world, exchangeable, communicable to other human beings, corruptible—and therefore truly a word indeed. Perhaps there can be no such thing as economic justice in a world which is actually embodied; for in such a world it is possible to give a gift—which is inherently unfair to those who did not get a gift—and to show mercy, which is inherently unjust and unequal.

What do we learn from this semantic analysis? First, obviously and syllogistically, that the issue of economic value is indeed bound up with the issue of meaning, reference, semantic value. Goods are valuable in rather the way words are meaningful. And the meaning of a piece of goods, as the meaning of a word, is what you desire it for. Wittgenstein said that if you want to know the meaning of a word, don't look at its definition, look at its use.

The pioneering investigator of human visual perception, David Marr, in his book *Vision* shows that the visual cortex does not "present to us what is there;" what is there depends on how it is constructed by the visual cortex. But the cortex only gives us a sort of menu of what we might want to notice; and serves up what, for our given purpose, is most functional. In other words, our senses are function-driven, controlled by the mental "mouse" of attention, which is moved by desire. We have a word for something because we have a reason to attend to it rather than the nine trillion other things we might make leap into reality by selectively attending to them; and we put an economic value on something because we have had the originality to notice it as desirable, or someone else has had that originality for us.

The second thing we learn is that value can be created internally, by means of a complication, unification, and densifying of the information field to the point where it becomes reflexive, and therefore generative of original novelty. A very simple system, for instance one with only one element, cannot produce meaning because it cannot generate anything beyond itself. A somewhat more complex system, with orderly rules, like the game of tic tac toe, may be capable of generating several states but it is essentially deterministic— that is, its states can be counted and defined in advance by any calculator more complex than it is, and the order of their appearance can be predicted. It is, therefore, not generative of original novelty. A system not bound by orderly rules is not a system, and can be reduced to an ensemble of independent and sterile simple systems. But if an orderly and rule-governed system is complex enough, it will cross a threshold beyond which no conceivable calculator could predict its future states, or at least predict them fast enough to outstrip their actual occurrence. At this point such a system is the most efficient predictor of its own future state, and takes on the qualities of reflexivity, autonomy, original generativeness, meaning, and value.

This theoretical analysis of system types, interestingly enough, recapitulates the actual progress of evolution, from the almost sterile simplicity of the Big Bang through the largely deterministic systems of physical and chemical evolution, to the rich generativeness of life and the still richer creativity, autonomy, and meaning of human culture.

Language is a system of the last kind, one with too many states to be counted and predicted, and thus a generative one. Its richest value-creating mode is poetry. Poetry is the place where the maximum connectivity and richest rules of language are permitted. It is the purest and most perfect form of economic activity, for its raw materials are utterly valueless and its product is the most expensive of all commodities: what is known as a literary education.

The position I have taken here with regard to the way in which value can be generated by complex systems should be carefully distinguished from such literary theories as the New Criticism and Structuralism. Such theories assume that literature is a closed system, whose internal structure is itself sufficient to generate literary value. They are like economic theories which contain no goods or creators of goods or consumers, but only financial instruments, bonds, currency, legal rules, and mathematical ratios. By cutting off literature in this way from the rest of Nature such theories deprive literature of its significance as part of the leading edge of universal evolution, as the mutating DNA, so to speak, of cultural organisms of exquisite protean beauty.

It is at the level where the relationships of words and sentences become so complex as to be reflexive and generative that the language system links up with the achieved integrated complexity of physical nature, and creatively interferes with it. (Deconstruction, because it attacks the rulegovernedness of such systems—no integrated complexity could survive its corrosive sarcoma long enough to begin generating reflexive and autonomous realities—has nothing to say about meaning and value. The value of Deconstruction is that it indeed says Nothing in a very striking and stimulating way.)

The complication of the information field which results in *meaning* in language and *means* in economics produces a hierarchical arrangement of values; and this is the third conclusion we can draw from a semantic analysis of the idea of value. The lowest values consist of mere tropisms, attractions and repulsions, positives and negatives. "It's good because I want it." Such valuations are binary or two-valued, that is, they are like switches, with only two positions, on and off. Although such valuations are not numerical or quantitative in themselves, they can be measured in the mass by such devices as statistical counts, polls, and voting.

The advantage of this kind of valuation is that not only all human beings are capable of it, but all animals as well. The disadvantages are obvious: extreme imprecision, and the complete absence of objectivity, predictive power, reflexive self-criticism, self-adjustment, and the possibility of negotiation. Moreover, such tropisms are contentless in themselves; they are only the result of the interplay of other, more articulate desires. Without the explicit mediating presence of other values, such as those of democratic due process, which would require a vote, the only way in which the differing desires of different individuals at this level can be reconciled is by conflict and the destruction of the weaker.

Nor is voting as unproblematic a way of ascertaining the will of the people as one might think. Consider three candidates in a primary election: Smith, who supports job creation at the expense of river pollution; Jones, who supports clean water and public health at the expense of higher taxes; and Brown, who supports lower taxes at the expense of job programs. It is quite possible that in one-to-one runoffs, Smith might defeat Jones, Jones might defeat Brown, and Brown might defeat Smith. The mathematician Condorcet and many modern followers have shown that voting can always produce paradoxes, such as the case where a majority of a voting population prefers A over B, B over C, and C over A. Voting is not necessarily commutative, as the logicians put it.

Somewhat more sophisticated are those values which express themselves in a graduated and quantitative way, which can be compared against each other in an individual case and expressed quantitatively. "It's good because I want it; but at five dollars you don't get as much of it as this other." In other words, economic value. For this kind of value, money is the ideal expression, for the price someone is prepared to pay for something exactly expresses its value in this sense. The numerical exhausts the expressive power of this type of value system.

Among the advantages of money valuation is that it is common to all human beings—indeed it is the highest value which can be reliably ascertained across different cultures and belief-systems. When two persons, it may be from the ends of the earth, agree on the price of something that one wishes to sell and the other to buy, no power on earth has more validity than that contract in establishing this kind of value. Moreover, unlike voting, it does not produce Condorcet's problems of commutativity.

Economic value is the most democratic of all forms of value. If we would have a political system that dispenses with the market and with money, then we must have one that is not democratic, and which must perforce be totalitarian in its control of all human exchange, lest genuine prices begin to be established. Most people are uncertain about the value of things in higher terms—their beauty, their truth, or their ethical goodness. And when they are certain, there is often deep conflict between them. The only environment in which the convinced can negotiate these issues with each other is one in which they are protected from each other—for they should properly be fanatical about their values—by the easygoing philistinism of the marketplace. This is why the market economy, the democratic regime, and the practice of philosophy always appear together.

Above economic value we find what we might call truth value. "It's good because, despite my desires, it is consistent with the truth." It was the heroic ambition of Enlightenment Europe to establish Universal Human Reason on as broad a base as economic value, so that Mankind (I use the masculine noun advisedly) might be united in a higher and nobler fashion than by trade and currency standards. What might that ideal have offered?—all the democratic advantages of economic valuations, but without their arbitrariness. Reason would have provided objective tests of economic valuations, and would have offered the virtues of negotiability and intelligibility—for reason would not be based on an inexplicable "black box" of desire. But alas, that vision failed; it is the tragedy of the last two centuries that it did so. Swift's reasonable Houyhnhnms, and their Nazi pogroms against the unreasonable but human Yahoos, are a tragic and ghastly foretaste of that failure.

Why did it fail? For four reasons. If "reasonable" means "logically coherent," the mathematician Gödel would tell us that no logical system is capable of proving its own truth. If "reasonable" means "consistent with the evidence," the philosopher Popper would tell us that the meaning of evidence includes falsifiability—that which we know on the basis of evidence is necessarily hostage to the possibility of counter-evidence. A third reason for the collapse of Reason was its encounter with other cultures, with apparently different canons of truth, worldviews, laws of what constitutes evidence, and criteria of logical coherency. A last reason was that Reason did not take into account the irreducible role of the observer in the reality being observed; there could be no absolute objectivity.

Despite these problems, a coherent view of the universe as including its observers, as generated by their disagreements, and as evolving through its very incapacity to calculate its own future states, is emerging. But this universe refers outside the realm of reason and truth to the higher realms of active human moral and aesthetic choice, and to the lower probabilistic propensity of objects in the world to collectively negotiate a crude consensus about reality, rather like a market economy. In fact it begins to look as if every level of our value hierarchy is necessary to sustain a satisfactory description of the world.

Historically the value of moral goodness—"It's good because it's good"—has struggled with the value of truth for primacy among the higher human values. Moral goodness, as a value, has many advantages. Unlike the value of Reason, it does not require systematic skepticism, and it easily translates into action, whereas truth by itself has a tendency, so to speak, to sit there and suggest nothing at all in the way of doing.

The great problem with moral goodness is that there is no way of deciding which version of it is better; in itself it is non-negotiable. The genius of Christianity, as of its heresy Communism, is that it proposes Love as its highest value, which seems to solve the problem by enjoining us to love one another like brothers; perhaps negotiation is not necessary. But suppose—and this is perfectly consistent—the best way we can love our errant brother is by burning him at the stake to save his soul, or the best way we can love human society is by killing all the bourgeoisie? Morality becomes tolerable only when it is hampered by democratic vote, a free market, and a constitution designed to protect "immoral" minorities.

But there are signs of hope that moral values may one

day be less arbitrary and more negotiable than they are today. Already the outlines of a set of universal moral rules, based on an understanding of human nature, is beginning to emerge from the study of neuropsychology, evolution, mammal and primate ethology, and comparative anthropology. What are those rules?

We can learn from neuropsychology to avoid conditions which stress, overload, or bore the nervous system; we can train our "hardwired" capacities for seeing other people's point of view; we can promote those practices of ritual, meditation, and so on, that stimulate the brain chemistry of social harmony. From the general strategy of survival in the world of biological evolution we may learn that adaptability and a concern for the future of the species, especially our young, are positive values; that promiscuous sex can lead to epidemic diseases; that any social institution, such as education, art, and mental discipline, which makes possible the imaginative construction of coherent and plausible internal models of the world—especially alternate models, with ways of testing them against each other and against the evidence—should be encouraged. The smarter and more adaptable we are, the more likely we are to survive.

We can at least be good mammals, and good primates, even if we are not sure how to be good human beings. A moral system, as the critic Alexander Argyros acutely points out, should at least be consistent with its own evolution. We learn from our close animal relatives that we must above all protect, nurture, and love our children through their first five years; that we must not kill a submissive enemy; that we should use only ritualized formal combat for resolving social disputes, and otherwise should accept a flexible and easygoing ranking system; that we should cooperate with each other; and that we are by nature gregarious and need to be cuddled and stroked and groomed by each other from time to time. Unfortunately, such a study gives us no guidance on whether killing is bad in itself, or on the value of sexual equality, or on the evils of war, rape, racism, lying, greed, and incest, all of which are common practices among our close animal relatives.

From cross-cultural anthropology we can learn other facts about our nature which may help us in the construction of a non-arbitrary and negotiable moral system. Incest is wrong, for instance; gifts are good, and we should ritualize our major life-crises. Disputes should be settled within a social framework. Killing is permissible only under special circumstances. Everybody should have some kind of religion, though religions are so various that secular humanism and materialism more than satisfy the minimum conditions for being called religions. We have property rights and personal rights, but their only universal feature is that they should be consistently and publicly upheld. Sexual morality, given a hygienic taboo on promiscuity and a stable system of child care, is almost infinitely various; consistency in adherence to the local code is the guiding principle. But human practice gives us no guidance in such matters as war, racial and sexual equality, religious tolerance, or environmental and ecological ethics, and would seem to cast doubt on some of the democratic values of equality, individualism, and freedom of speech. Most of the United Nation's "human rights" have no universal warrant in human practice: those rights are a fragile and precious achievement of civilization, not a natural inheritance.

One major problem with all "nature"-based value-systems is that evolution itself took a giant leap forward when it gave rise to us human beings. By virtue of our enormously enhanced capacities for learning from individual experience and for the original creation of new worldviews, we entered into a dialectic with our own nature. With the aid of our traditional arts and rituals we came to understand, to accept, to manipulate, and thus partly to transcend the biological constraints that bind us and our animal relatives. Later science helped us to escape the technological constraints which limit traditional societies—our inability to control our environment and our fertility, our medical ignorance, our vulnerability to famine, and our murderous incomprehension of other cultures than our own. But some of us, in consequence of our scientific liberation from these constraints, came to believe that we had no nature at all, and could thus afford to neglect the traditional moral and aesthetic disciplines by which we had gained some measure of control over it.

Moreover a morality based on our nature, as any Kantian ethicist would point out, is not in itself ethical at all, but merely prudential. Likewise, a morality constituted by the will of an omnipotent Lawgiver. Why is the Lawgiver's will good? Moralists, if pressed, must fall back on such aesthetic concepts as fairness or moral beauty. Morality must always refer outside its own sphere for justification, and thus fall hostage to other values than moral ones.

Beauty may turn out to be in some ways the most reliable of values. "It's good because it's beautiful" makes a good deal of sense. It is not only the seekers of moral goodness who fall back on aesthetic criteria when forced to justify their choices; the scientist and the philosopher, the seekers of the good defined as the true, must also concede a central role to beauty. Any set of evidence can justify an infinite range of explanatory hypotheses, each of which can be self-consistent and cover all the facts. Finally, scientists and philosophers choose one theory over another because it is simply more beautiful, more "elegant," as they say.

The chief advantage of beauty as a value is that it need not refer outside itself, as must morality, truth, and economic value; and it generates its own ineffabilities at its borders. Beauty is the organizing principle which governs the incipient, incalculable, and unpredictable coming into being of the universe in each new moment. It is thus eternal, in that it always rises a moment before the wave of concrescence that we experience as the present moment; and it is by the same token as evanescent as the rainbow that floats over the falls.

Beauty, moreover, does not seem to arouse those energies of terrified, insecure, and absolute belief that make moral goodness so bloody a banner in the history of humankind. Beauty makes no Jihads or Crusades, though it is too often the victim of them. And beauty does seem to have certain pan-cultural characteristics, that are now being explored by those whom I have called the natural classicists. The sensation of beauty is regarded by them as the brain reward for our most characteristically human activity, the construction of plausible integrations of information into possible future universes. It arose, I believe, out of ritual activity—collective dreaming—which originally acted as a selective pressure upon our genes so as to produce the creative, educable, and free animal the ritual demanded.

But the aesthetic, too, has its problems. Of all the value systems it is the one which is the least accessible to the great mass of the population (especially in its higher forms), the hardest to learn, the slowest to become established in a culture, and the easiest to stereotype and thus to denature. Almost everybody has some capacity for the experience of beauty; but the extent and subtlety of that capacity varies much more greatly even than intelligence, and beauty's quiet voice is easily drowned out by the strident hollering of political interest and economic desire. A value system based on aesthetics would be radically aristocratic.

We have, then, exhausted the known value systems: the tropic—as I suppose one might call that system which defines the good as what one desires—the economic, the philosophic, the moral, and the aesthetic. None of them is sufficient by itself to provide us with a reliable basis of value.

The one which is internally most perfect, and most necessary to the meaning of the others—the aesthetic—demands
capacities that are the least widely shared; and it is the
slowest to determine, taking centuries to become established
in a cultural canon. The most paradigmatic one, and the one
which demands our fiercest allegiance—moral goodness—is
tragically non-negotiable. The most objective one—Truth—
is logically inconsistent in itself. The most negotiable and
most democratic one—economic value—is not satisfying to
our higher capacities and has no way of accounting for its
own content. In fact its content must be a numerical reduction of all the higher values, without which its bottom line—
price and profit—would mean nothing. Mere tropism—the
good as what I desire—begs the whole question, since my
desire is compounded of all the others; and it is non-negotiable, completely lacking in objectivity, and impossible to determine collectively in any precise way.

But perhaps the wisdom of those words we analyzed—
"good," "mean," "interest," and so on—is that we must see
value as essentially composite, hierarchical, contextual, and
constructed. The higher values depend on the lower values
for their expression, incarnation in the world, propagation,
and development. The lower values depend on the higher
values for their meaning, content, organization, and identification. The crucial link is economic value, which is the
lingua franca the others must speak if they are to speak at
all in the community of human beings.

No pure values will suffice. An economic decision which
ignores the aesthetic is not just a bad economic decision, it
is one without content and thus paradoxically levels a blow
at the very economics it is designed to exploit. For instance,
big publishers and Hollywood studios which persistently
issue derivative and market-researched material, while temporarily enlarging their market share, will eventually dry
up the pool of their readers or audience, and in the long run

contribute to economic inflation—less real bang for the buck. Likewise, businesses which undermine or break the spirit of morality, or which ignore scientific fact, will sooner or later come to grief, while contributing to the decline of the economy of which they are a part.

But the corollary is also true. A social welfare policy which persists in violating the essential nature of money— that is, exchange—will, however moral its aims, destroy the process by which money itself acquires value. It will thus damage those whom it wishes to help, in the most horrible way—by pushing them outside the democracy of the marketplace and consigning them to the dim realm of those for whom the good is merely one's own private desires. Economically, this effect shows up both as high unemployment and as inflation.

Equally disastrous are the attempts of the moral to regulate the claims of truth or beauty by censorship, as the Moral Majority on the right and the liberal opponents of sociobiology on the left have tried to do with evolution. Similarly, an avant-garde artist who ignores or flouts the claims of morality, or scientific truth, or the marketplace, or the simple human need for gratification—or all of them—cannot produce work of any value. And a scientist who, in pursuit of objective truth, denied the moral, the aesthetic, or the economic would, if by some miracle allowed to do science at all, do bad science. For the components of the world draw their identity from one another, as quantum physics shows; and thus a truth torn away from that whole system which includes choosing observers would be no truth at all.

The miracle of value really works, and it produces realities which are as objective as anything else in this gloriously, if disquietingly, tentative universe. But it works only when its full hierarchy is in place. The specialization which has enabled us to discover so much about the universe in the last four hundred years, by dividing off the experts and devotees of the market, truth, morality, and beauty from one another, had the deadly side-effect of almost murdering the unity of the world and thus the integrity of the human psyche. In a sense the hydrogen bomb was the concrete expression of that danger.

But if we are to restore that unity, we must be prepared for marriages of ideas, compromises, and contradictions that may gravely bewilder us and question many of our deepest assumptions. The clearest and strongest way of putting this is to assert the need for the copresence of justice and mercy, payment and gifts, merit and luck, the determinate and the indeterminate in the workings of our new unified value system. As two opposites—mutation, which is random and irrational, and selection, which is ordered and rational—are required to make evolution work, so these dialectical opposites are required for the healthy and creative functioning of a value system.

Let us examine the implications of this. As I have already hinted, a merciful act is one which by definition cannot be fully accounted for by the merits of the recipient of it. If it were, then it would not be mercy but plain justice. If everybody is treated with equal mercy, then again that treatment would be a form of justice, not mercy—the ground rules of justice would simply have been changed, that is all. So mercy is necessarily undeserved and necessarily unequal.

Yet consider a world without mercy; as Portia says in *The Merchant of Venice,* "The quality of mercy is not strained;/ It droppeth like the gentle rain of heaven/ Upon the place beneath . . ." A world without mercy would be a desert, and we would be confronted so absolutely with our own failings at every moment that our lives would be unendurable. There is no need to doubt that the just man sins the Biblical seventy times seven times a day. Such a world would have no tolerances; scales would have to weigh their meat to the last fraction of an atom's weight, even when matter itself, because of its blessed quantum inexactness, comes in an irreducible texture that cannot be reduced, or strained, to use Portia's punning metaphor, any further. What "gentleness" could there be in such a world? What partiality to one's lover, one's brother, one's children, those with whom we are "gently" or genitally, or kindly, or kindredly, connected? Such a world could have no liquids or gases in it, only solids at zero degrees on the Kelvin scale.

And yet mercy can be terribly cruel to those who deny it and who insist on justice, and to those who are not lucky enough to get it. A world of pure mercy would be utterly arbitrary, subject to the whims of whoever had the lucky talent to create the goods that others desire. Shylock is a tragic figure, and Shylock has been protected from the full cruelty of mercy by the law. Without Venetian justice, such as it is, he might long ago have been torn to pieces by a Christian mob which objected to his mercilessness. There are deep ironies, as Marc Shell points out in his book *The Economy of Literature,* in Shakespeare's punning connections among the words "ius," the Latin for "law;" "iewes," the Elizabethan for "Jews;" as well as "use," the taking of interest, and "ewes," the sacrificial animals that Jacob's divinely just luck wins away from Laban.

Or consider Oedipus, who lives in a world which truly does operate at the whimsical mercy of the gods. His act of self-blinding is heroic precisely because it denies that his terrible history is bad luck, and insists that it was his own fault and responsibility, and punishes him accordingly. In punishing himself Oedipus wrests the moral initiative from the gods, and makes their mercy and their play seem pretty shabby. There is an irreducible human grandeur in the notion that we should justly deserve what is meted out to us; and that ideal has been responsible for some of the most glorious chapters in human social history—the assault on tyranny, the abolition of slavery, the creation of trades unions, the attack on racism and sexism.

But we cannot abolish luck, hazard, mercy, free gifts,

the indeterminate. It is their realm which constitutes the evolutionary potential of the species, our future, that which the universe-calculator has not yet got around to figuring out and thus has not yet happened. It is the inside of those riddling and gnomic caskets whose meaning is the fertile womb of woman, or the grave; and all the luck of privileged or talented—or monstrous, or handicapped—birth.

So for good to exist, for value to be created, we must endure a world which agonizingly combines the rule of two supreme but warring authorities—justice and mercy. We must become accustomed to that double bind, knowing that any attempt to replace the world's brutal justice with mercy leads to the hell of arbitrary tyranny, while to try by revolution to institute universal social justice must lead to the still more horrible hell of the Gulag and the killing fields. Life is unfair, and it ought to be fair; but it ought also to be unfair. In other words, the only workable theory of value is a tragic theory.

Perhaps the paradox can be made more endurable by noting that if things are as they ought to be, then any change, any becoming, must be a declension and a descent from that perfection; and since life is a process of change a fortiori, then if life is to go on there ought to be a difference between what is and what ought to be. But if there is such a difference, then what ought to be is indeed so; and the paradox deepens into a reflexive maelstrom rather reminiscent of the actual protean energy of things as they really unfold. Perhaps we must be content with a world of value in which we never encounter smooth surfaces or integer relations, but always fractal dimensions, pitted and frilled with the attempt to reach perfection, and complications which always approach but do not quite achieve simplicity.

If this is so, then the most dangerous and self-destructive trait we have is our expectation of purity and unadulteratedness in matters of value. How wise is Jane Austen when she has her heroine Elizabeth Bennet reflect, on seeing her unrequited lover's magnificent country house, that it would be something to be mistress of Pemberley. What any Romantic moralist would condemn as a gross defilement of motive, we must now see as a sign of extraordinary psychic health. Elizabeth is still perfectly capable of turning Darcy down, and she does so again a few pages later. But she has been able to include material and economic interests in her value decisions, without allowing them to rule over other considerations properly higher in the hierarchy.

We may see that same wholeness in the much disputed last act of *The Merchant of Venice,* where, oblivious to the recent destruction of Shylock's very being, Lorenzo and Jessica, young and beautiful parasites, the recipients of undreamed of luck and wealth and happiness, contemplate the floor of Heaven, thick inlaid with patines of bright gold, and listen to the music of the spheres. Shakespeare is aware of the fate of Shylock, but the beauty of his poetry is not oppressed by its muddy vesture of decay. Evolutionarily, we are all, like Lorenzo and Jessica, the survivors of a history of imperfect justice; and we need strong stomachs to know what we are made of.

The caskets of *The Merchant of Venice,* and Elizabeth's marriage-choice, both have reference to the mysterious work of a woman's womb. The sign of the true lover is that he is able to find his beloved's body as beautiful and as dense with her intoxicating spirit after he has seen it in childbirth, with the great dangling purple entrails of umbilicus and placenta being pulled forth from her body. In fact, the true lover is the tenderer and the more astonished by the miracle of her personal being. Value is constructed out of its own evolutionary history, and its golden meaning is a comic and tragic transmutation of baser metal.

# TEMPEST,
# FLUTE & OZ

COGNITIVE SCIENCE—THAT NEW DIS-
cipline embracing elements of neuroanat-
omy, neurochemistry, perceptual psychology, anthropology, mathematics, philosophy, linguistics, and computer science—is
finding that intelligence is not a passive
processor of input but a force of active interference with the
world and with itself. We interrogate the world according to
a prearranged action-pattern which provides our questions
with purpose and relevance.

In other words, we need a *story,* a connected series of
projected or fictional actions with a beginning, middle, and
end, in order to make sense of the world. We compare our
immediate experience and our memory of what has gone
before with the story, and so locate ourselves in a map which

provides a present moment, a "here," surrounded by a past
and a future. We can identify the significant causal features
of our situation, anticipate what will happen next, and de-
cide on what to do about it. Plans arise out of stories, as a
chosen direction of action within the story-space. Sensory
experience now acquires a focus, a means to edit the enormous, brain-stunning volume of input to reveal significant
features and shapes. When the result corresponds with what
the story predicts, we can go on with more confidence in our
plan; when it contradicts the story, we can switch to a series
of meta-stories, including the stories of refining, calibrating,
and reinterpreting the sensory input, rewriting the story, or
choosing a new story from the personal or cultural repertoire.

Science itself, from this point of view, is a huge new body
of stories, all connected with each other, with scenarios
called hypotheses, action-plans called experiments, and
goals such as mathematical simplicity, logical coherence,
empirical accuracy, predictive power, elegance, and richness. Science, in turn, fits into larger stories, concerning the
intellectual and spiritual fulfilment of the scientist, the expansion of the power and knowledge of humankind, the need
of the universe for an appreciative observer, or the greater
glory of God.

Certain very large stories orient, contain, and govern
the smaller stories which constitute the archive of human
plans. They are called myths. They are essential to a culture,
and their health and vitality affect the fabric of ordinary life
in the most pervasive way. This is not to say that ideological
conformity is good for a society. In fact, some of the most
invigorating myths are meta-myths about the rejection of
prior myths: the American myth of its revolution, for instance, or the Renaissance myth of the questioning of theo-
logical authority, or the Greek myths of the overthrow of
earlier generations of gods. The health of a myth depends

partly on its capacity to adapt to changes in the smaller stories of which it is composed, which in turn may have been necessitated by encounters with unassimilable and obdurate experience. Moreover, there are even myths of the value of a plurality of myths; polytheism is one kind of pluralist myth, and the American narrative of the democratic process is another.

But there comes a point where the limits of a myth's flexibility are reached, where it breaks; or it is set aside, to remain intact but unexposed to the lifegiving stream of experience. If there is nothing to replace the myth, then there is no way of interrogating experience, and experience itself begins to dry up: the population of a society that has lost its myths literally becomes less intelligent, for myths are the tools of intelligence.

In the Renaissance the Christian myth proved so intractable—producing irresolvable religious wars and stifling scientific and technological progress—that it was set aside from the flow of experience. Hence, the separation of Church and State. Hence also, the allocation of the empirical world of sensory experience to science, and the creation of an abstract, non-sensory spiritual world where the Christian myth could be kept safe. Despite outbreaks of anomie such as we find depicted in *Hamlet* and Dürer's woodcut of Melancholy, the Renaissance generated powerful new myths to replace the old—of progress, nation, human aspiration, exploration, wealth, science itself.

But when an old myth cannot be adequately replaced, a society suffers some deep damage and loses its capacity to contribute to the rest of the world. Often, then, it is swallowed up by a larger culture with vital stories of its own, as Athens was by the empires of Macedonia and Rome when its myths failed in the Peloponnesian Wars. If the collapse of the myths is sufficiently total, as among the Ik, the demoralized African tribe described by Colin Turnbull, the fundamental familial and personal structures themselves break down, and human beings become recognizably less valuable to each other than animals are. Contemporary critics of culture and the arts sometimes unthinkingly assume that freedom consists in liberation from all myths; but myths can be the foundation of freedom, providing the subjunctive space within which creative alternatives to the mills of event and instinct become possible.

Not all myths honor creative invention, however. One enduring myth, for instance, concerns the dangers of innovation, especially in science and technology. (I use "myth" in a broad sense, so that we can see the same essential structure reemerging again and again over the centuries.) The heart of this myth is that a foolish and prideful person discovers some deep and powerful source of knowledge and power; he or she explores that knowledge and uses that power; but it goes wrong, and the divine authorities strike down the transgressor with a horrible punishment.

There are many versions of this myth, or perhaps, more accurately, this "mytheme" or mythic motif. The story of Adam and Eve and the Fall contains it. So also the Greek stories of Pandora, Prometheus, Phaeton, and Icarus. It crops up more recently in *The Sorcerer's Apprentice, Frankenstein,* and *Faust* (though Goethe turns the latter on its head). It has remained essentially untouched by the great transitions from polytheism through monotheism to contemporary environmentalism. It expresses the fear that human aspiration will bring about catastrophes, pollutions, a humbling of human pride by divine or natural punishment. We find it, vulgarized, in the phrase "Don't mess with Mother Nature."

The myth perhaps represents the regulative side of the priestly or Brahmin caste, its defense against innovation and change, especially changes instigated by its own initiates or postulants in the course of their instruction. In the broadest sense it is an attempt to prevent the cultural inheritance of myth from branching out into new stories, either by denying the legitimate succession of the new stories, or by threats of punishment or horrible consequences for those who carry the new stories on. The priestly persecutors of Galileo and Bruno were acting out the myth; and we find it in our own time in the Scopes trial, and more recently in the attacks that have been made against sociobiology, technology, evolution, and genetic engineering.

But there is another myth, still in the process of articulating itself, which can already, I believe, act as a generous and freeing guide to our future. Although it has cropped up in many versions, most notably in science fiction, the three best examples of it are Shakespeare's *The Tempest,* Mozart's *The Magic Flute* (especially Ingmar Bergman's inspired film version), and the well-known MGM movie *The Wizard of Oz* (1939). Who are the central characters of the myth, and what is its story?

First, of course, there is the Wizard. He is impressive at first, even terrifying; but unlike the divine authority figures of the Sorcerer's Apprentice myth, he is less terrifying than he pretends to be. All three wizards love to show off their magical illusions in masque or spectacle, and are rather vain about them; but they are under no illusions about the real importance of their tricks (except as an inducement to virtue). They are wealthy—they "prosper"—but care nothing for their wealth, knowing it to be an illusion created by the desire to possess what one thinks is desirable, because one imagines that others desire it and that they experience a plentitude of being when they possess it. The Wizard is frankly relieved when the illusion is revealed as such, for the strain of maintaining it is becoming a nuisance. Because Stephano and Trinculo cannot make these discriminations, they can be distracted from mayhem by the gorgeous stage-costumes hung on the lime-tree, and are, like birds, limed by them. Caliban is wiser than his "civilized" masters and knows trash when he sees it. But still, the Wizard is human enough to enjoy his own conjuring tricks.

"Pay no attention to that man behind the curtain," says Dr. Marvel when his awesome masquerade is unveiled by the little dog Toto; but when Dorothy confronts him and accuses him of being a bad man, he retorts with some justice that he is a good man, but a bad wizard. In a sense, The Great And Powerful Oz is a fraud, but upon that fraud is based the peace, freedom, and prosperity of the Emerald City. And as we shall see, the conferral of fraudulent, or let us say factitious, honors such as a diploma of thinkology and a medal of valor can paradoxically validate a real spiritual achievement. There is a great mystery here, at the heart of the myth, to which we must return.

Although Sarastro and Prospero are less fallible, there are hints in both their characters that they not only have failings but know them very well. In Ingmar Bergman's film version the endearing humanity of Sarastro—his underestimation of the corruption and violence of Monostatos, his slackness in disciplining Papageno, his inability to fully conceal his resentment at being rejected by his wife, the Queen of Night, his weariness with authority and desire to hand it over to the young people—is emphasized by details like the frayed glove of one of his lieutenants, which touchingly reveals a gnarled knuckle.

Prospero, like Sarastro, underestimates the threat posed by Caliban until it is almost too late. He is preoccupied, absent-minded, quick-tempered, and increasingly tired. He thinks more and more of his own death. Though he acts the part of the terrifying authority figure in forcing the Prince Ferdinand to carry logs, and in forbidding his daughter to speak to her lover, he does so for the express purpose of eliciting rebellion from his over-dependent daughter and courageous sacrifice from the spoiled young Prince. Unlike

the God of the Old Testament, he wants his Adam and Eve
to disobey him, and rewards them when they do.

Prospero recognizes his own moral limits; he knows that
he cannot redeem the natures of his brother Sebastian and
Antonio, and that he must use blackmail to keep them from
evildoing. Of Caliban he says, "This thing of darkness I acknowledge mine;" and the withdrawn suggestion that he is
in some ways Caliban's father—and is thus, metaphorically,
the dark moon-god Setebos and husband of the Witch Sycorax—is an act of moral genius that can only come from the
deepest knowledge and acceptance of his own faults. It is also
a moment of mythic insight that is to be taken up and developed in Bergman's version of *The Magic Flute,* in which
Sarastro is indeed the ex-husband of the Witch, the moon-
goddess and Queen of the Night.

Either symbolically or actually, then, the Wizard is the
husband of the Witch and the father of the young Princess.
In *The Wizard of Oz,* the problem of how to make the Wizard
into Dorothy's father is solved by making her an orphan
being brought up by her aunt and uncle. Dr. Marvel, the
Wizard and transitional figure between Kansas and Oz, can
thus step into the role of father while keeping a flavor of
magic, power, and charlatanry that would be inappropriate
in a Kansas farmer. The fact that Dorothy inherits the red
shoes from the Wicked Witch, whose twin sister becomes her
inveterate enemy, is a lucid piece of dream- and myth-logic
suggesting that the Witch is the absent mother. Thus, some
of the hidden energy that makes the film so unforgettable
comes from the tacit implication that Oz and the Witch/
schoolteacher are ex-lovers!

The Wizard's powers unite four elements, often held by
earlier myths to be separate: an abstract and sublime personal and political ethic; the scientific and philosophical investigation of nature, with an attendant technological power
over it; all the tricks, deceits, lovely illusions and manipula-

tions of art; and the magical powers of the sorcerer. Victor
Peterson, in a brilliant unpublished essay, argues that for
Shakespeare magic was the prime symbol of the intensification and evolution of time, by which consciousness and
spirit—that "cunning'st pattern of excelling nature," as
Othello puts it—emerge out of the lower and more material
levels of reality. In *The Tempest,* magic—Prospero's art, his
magician's mantle and actor's costume—can be said to sum-
marize goodness, truth, beauty, and power into a single dynamic and creative idea. But it is always done very lightly:
the magician is something of a stage manager or playwright,
and though he commands powerful forces of nature they are
often, like theatrical talent, temperamental, unruly, and in-
dependent-minded.

"Sarastro" is a version of Zoroaster or Zarathustra, who
preached the gospel of Ahura-Mazda, the god of light. The
Wizard is in general associated with light and reason, even
if the light is only a fiction. In Prospero's name we find
prosperity—the Wizard unashamedly and justly commands
great riches, even though he lives in a simple cell. We also
find hope, "spero": the Wizard is one who through all the
bitter experience of his life has never become a cynic and has
preserved his idealism for the future. He is one who has not
ceased to "marvel," which is the earthly name of the Wizard
of Oz.

The role of the Wizard is to instruct and test the young
heroine, his daughter, by a series of ordeals. (Though
Pamina is not Sarastro's daughter in the original *Flute,*
Bergman responds to the pressure of the myth and makes
her his daughter in his own film version.) He must also test
the hero, when there is one, but the hero is somewhat less
important, as his absence from *The Wizard of Oz* attests. The
new myth has taken several decisive steps beyond the ancient monomyth that Joseph Campbell describes in his su-
perb *Hero With a Thousand Faces.* One of them is the new

role of the heroine as an active and dynamic source of events. As in many science-fiction stories, in which the Mad Scientist has a beautiful daughter, the Wizard's daughter is quite as likely to inherit his power as is the less interesting son-in-law.

As central to the myth as the Wizard himself is the Beast-Man that is his opposite, foil, and shadow. The Beast-Man is one of the mythic fundamentals. He appears as Enkidu, the Minotaur, Polyphemus, Grendel; is interestingly absent in Biblical and Christian myth, unless Jesus himself, born in a manger and nourished in the desert on locusts and wild honey, is a disguised example; but he is a staple of the old fairytales and is found in the gargoyles of cathedrals. He reappears in the Renaissance as the noble savages of Rabelais, Montaigne and, later, Rousseau, and in such figures as the Wild Boy of Aveyron; in the nineteenth and twentieth centuries his avatars are everywhere: Frankenstein, Mr. Hyde, Freud's Id, Mowgli, and Tarzan, among others.

He is our predecessor, the cave man, from whom we inherited the island of our nature and talents, but whose brutishness we fear and must reject. The Tempest/Flute/Wizard myth makes use of him in a new way. In *The Tempest,* he is Caliban, of course, but he also appears more subtly as the nature-spirit Ariel; in *Flute,* he is divided into the good Papageno and Papagena and the bad Monostatos. In *Wizard,* he has interestingly fissioned, in a way which reflects the American experience, into several figures, including the Cowardly Lion (good, wild, natural man), the Winged Monkey Captain, (evil, wild, unnatural man), Toto (good, domesticated nature), the Scarecrow (good, artificial/natural man) and even, in a new development, the Tin Man, who to my mind is a mythic anticipation of Artificial Intelligence—good, domesticated, "unnatural" machine. (Dorothy's three friends also fulfill, as we shall see, the mythic roles of Folktale Helpers and magical spirit guides, and even act as partial substitutes for the absent Prince. Myth, like dream, is capable of remarkable economies and will happily collapse different functions into one another if it can get away with it.)

One curious problem raised by the Beast-Man is whether he is natural or artificial. The Minotaur was begotten by a bull upon Pasiphae using a technological simulation of a cow, and this element of the Beast-Man's mythic ancestry comes to signify the question whether the very notion of natural man is itself an artificial human construct—that is, perhaps there is something deeply wrong with the nature-culture distinction itself. Caliban is the result of an unnatural union, and the Scarecrow and Tin Man—and possibly the flying monkeys—are human constructions.

The Beast-Man is our ancestor, from whom we evolved. If he is our servant, he is sometimes a treacherous one. Caliban is the son of the Wicked Witch, and plots Prospero's death; Monostatos, ostensibly the servant of Sarastro, is in league with his enemy the Queen of Night. The myth versions are unanimous in suggesting that the Beast-Man is, in one of his aspects, a rapist; Caliban would "people all the isle with Calibans" begotten upon an unwilling Miranda; Monostatos would do the same thing to Pamina; and the Monkey King literally carries Dorothy off in his arms. Even when they are on the side of good, they are impulsive and tend to be victims of their fears and desires. The Lion is cowardly; the Scarecrow barely in control of his body. Papageno miserably fails Sarastro's tests of continence, and he and Papagena, in their glorious duet toward the end of the opera, clearly intend to people all the isle with little Papagenas and Papagenos. Their name means something like "daddy-maker" and they exemplify the healthy polyphiloprogenitiveness that is a key element in Darwin's theory of evolution. There is a faint suggestion that the Princess is attracted to the Beast-Man; he is thus a vital ingredient in the handsome Prince.

Even when the Beast-Man is bad, he has many appealing virtues. He can be a useful worker, hewing wood and drawing water; he has a certain common sense, and can sometimes distinguish the superficial aspects of the political system from its fundamentals better than can the depraved and addicted or idealistic and effete products of civilization. It is Toto who draws aside the curtain to reveal the conjurer at his tricks. The Beast-Man has poetic and musical gifts: he is given the magic bells, and recognizes as beautiful the sounds and sweet airs that give delight but hurt not. He knows where the fertile places and fresh springs are on the island. He is in fact the legitimate prior owner and natural sovereign of the island; the Wizard's claim to it can only be by right of annexation, and may only be temporary.

Like Bottom, in *A Midsummer Night's Dream,* the Beast-Man may wear an ass' head but he is also the only mortal to see the fairies as they are. When Peter Quince sees him metamorphosed and cries out, "Bless thee, Bottom, thou art translated," he is wiser than he knows: for the translation of Bottom is indeed ass. Perhaps significantly, Mozart's librettist and impresario Schikaneder had produced an *Oberon* immediately before the *Flute;* MGM had filmed the amazing Mickey Rooney version of *A Midsummer Night's Dream* shortly before the *Wizard;* and Bergman had his own *Smiles of a Summer's Night* in mind when he made his version of the opera. In many respects *The Tempest* is a completion, reversal, and restatement of *A Midsummer Night's Dream;* both deal with the beneficial use of imaginative power and magical technology; and both contain at their center the Beast-Man, the mooncalf, the man with the head of an ass, Bottom, who is at the bottom of our nature. This thing of darkness we acknowledge ours. The guilt we feel about the Beast-Man is justified, but we also feel oddly that we were right in oppressing him anyway. At least we will be right if we use for a greater good the powers we have usurped.

Another central figure in the myth is the Wicked Witch:

Sycorax, the Queen of Night, the Wicked Witch of the West. While the Wizard is usually associated with light—that is, with the knowable and verifiable—the Witch is associated with darkness and mystification. She is perhaps the ex-consort of the Wizard, and at least symbolically the mother of the Beast-Man. As the Beast-Man is associated with a controlling but uncontrolled male sexuality, the Witch is associated with a controlling but uncontrolled female sexuality. If the Beast-Man is natural man in its darkest and most retrograde aspect, the Witch is our whole mammalian inheritance from the rest of nature, also in its most dangerous form. While the Wizard represents freedom (which often comes in the forbidding guise of discipline and self-restraint), the Witch represents slavery, bondage, magic as motivational compulsion: the deterministic aspects of our physical nature.

But like Caliban and the other Beast-Men, the Witch has valuable and indispensable characteristics. She can confer gifts which, though they can be used properly only with the advice of the Wizard, are of great intrinsic value and are not necessarily corrupted by their source. In *The Wizard of Oz* some of the good aspects of the Witch are conferred on Glynda, the Good Witch; but the red slippers come from the Bad Witch, and it is by their agency alone, not by the male balloon of Dr. Marvel, that Dorothy is able to return home. A superficial reading of the myth might take the red shoes to represent female sexuality, but they mean far more than that. They are Dorothy's courage and creativeness and faith and capacity for achievement and love, just as the sword in a fairy tale will usually mean not only the male sexuality of the Prince but also his daring, magnanimity, purity of heart, and capacity for heroic action. In her avatar as Dorothy's schoolteacher, the Witch is Dorothy's "bad mother;" but from whom else but a mother might one inherit such slippers?

The imagery of the Witch stresses a certain circularity

in her nature. She is often silhouetted against the moon, and contained within its circle. Her nose and chin meet each other. Sycorax is "with age and envy. . .grown into a hoop." The problem with the Witch is that she goes round only in circles; she can make no progress. She is that in our nature which cannot break out of the natural cycle, to creativity and freedom and the meta-insights of reason. Her wheel can never become a helix or spiral or gyre, but can only repeat itself. She envies the higher powers that have grown out of and away from her, but she cannot grow with them or celebrate the freedom that they bring.

Though the myth requires that the Witch be rejected, it is remarkably generous in its allowance of her value and good offices. From Sycorax, Prospero inherits not only the island itself but also the services of the magical spirit Ariel. Tamino owes his very life to the Queen of Night, as in the first scene of the opera she and her minions rescue him from the Dragon. She punishes Papageno for lying, gives him the bells, gives Tamino the flute (though it was Sarastro who found the flute in the first place), and is the mother of the Princess.

Like the Beast-Man, she has a certain pathos; but she does not share the capacity for that pity (except for herself) that we and her victims can feel even for her. The light comprehendeth the darkness, but the darkness comprehendeth it not. Her powers are authentic in a way that the Wizard's sometimes are not; which implies that if we do not have faith in the Wizard, and keep up the "noble lie" of his legitimacy, the Emerald City and the holy halls of Sarastro may lose their freedom just as the Munchkins and the followers of Monostatos had lost theirs. Nevertheless, the Witch can be defeated by the simplest and most natural means, such as water, if the heart is pure and the moral intention to reject her temptation is held with courage.

Behind this dark female figure there can be dimly distinguished an even more terrifying and evil force, this time male, embodied in the tempest or tornado, perhaps representing the primal reptilian darkness out of which all of our ancestors came. In *The Tempest* he is Setebos, the moon-god, Sycorax's demon lover, and is further imaged forth in the storm at sea with which the play begins. In *The Magic Flute* he is the Dragon, again at the very beginning, which almost kills Tamino. In *Oz,* he is not personified, but we can sense his presence in the tornado at the beginning of the movie, and perhaps in the dark forest, among the malevolent trees.

But there are also beneficent spirits, forces, and magical helpers: Ariel and his rabble of fairy stagehands and actors; the boy spirits in *Flute;* and Dorothy's three friends in Oz. They are the Five Wits, the glorious unfallen powers and capacities of humankind, our heart, intelligence, courage, imagination, and spiritual hopefulness. They are also the source of our technological ingenuity; Bergman captures this well by giving the boy spirits in *Flute* a balloon (like Dr. Marvel's in Oz) from which to play their role as deus ex machina. In *The Tempest,* Ariel has a special care for the "royal, good, and gallant ship," the pride of Elizabethan technology; and as we have noted the Tin Man is an early robot or cyborg.

The cast of the myth also includes, of course, the young hero and heroine. As we have already noted, the hero is not strictly necessary, perhaps because the old myths of heroic achievement have already defined an acceptable path for the male as male. The new myth applies to both men and women, but is especially relevant to women in that it provides a new, more public role for them. In Oz, the folktale Helpers—the Straw Man and so on—must achieve an anagnorisis of their own, like Dorothy's, and their awakening serves instead of that of the absent Prince.

The central story of the myth is this: the Prince and/or Princess is saved from a natural catastrophe, associated with the ancient natural enemies of humankind. They may be saved by the Witch herself, or by the Wizard; but in any case the saving represents the terrible risks through which we human beings won through to our present physiological endowment and socio-technological security. Even our darkest powers and appetites served us well in that struggle to survive, and we should not be ungrateful to them, even if we must now subordinate them to higher values. The Prince and Princess learn of the Wizard, who seems at first to be a terrifying and tyrannical figure. They are at first under the power and sign of the Witch, who resents the usurpation of her land and the dispossession and enslavement of her son and servant, the Beast-Man, by her ex-consort the Wizard, and she wishes to use the Prince and Princess to regain her rightful domain over the human spirit. (In *The Tempest* Sycorax is represented in her absence by the temptation toward sexual license and mutual disrespect that Ferdinand and Miranda must overcome. That temptation closely resembles the field of poppies which attracts Dorothy from the true path.)

The deceits and evil intents of the Witch are revealed, sometimes in an attempt by her son the Beast-Man to rape the Princess, and unwillingly the hero and heroine accept the moral rightness of the Wizard's claims and the beauty of his spiritual world. The hero and heroine must now undergo a series of ordeals and tests imposed by the Wizard, during which they must repeat the evolutionary struggle that the whole human race had to pass through in the achievement of the higher moral virtues of love, honesty, self-control, insight into others, and acceptance of death. Bergman brings out the evolutionary implications of the ordeals by the suggestion of cave paintings in the passage where Tamino and Pamina pass through the fire and flood, protected by the playing of the flute. Shakespeare points a similar moral with the masque of spirits, which explains the ordeal in terms of the evolutionary replacement of lust by marriage. In Oz, the winged monkeys allude to the Darwinian descent of man.

The tests involve especially the capacity to remain silent: not to blurt out unthinkingly what is in one's head (the vice of Papageno) but to observe, restrain oneself, wait, think, reflect. Freedom consists in an internal feedback loop, which can only be established if the immediate connection between stimulus and response, sense-perception and expression, is temporarily broken. Freedom is an enlargement of the present moment. Only in this way may an interval be made between irrevocable past and predetermined future, an interval or delay in which a whole universe of intention and creative decision can be created. Prospero self-deprecatingly describes his masque of spirits as a mere vanity of his art, a pastime, to while away the time before the nuptials. But like his modesty, which implies a capacity for silence, the masque's function of delay is of fundamental importance. The tests imply the deferral of sexual desire, and thus the establishment of a mode of sexuality beyond the prehuman norm of mutual rape.

Deferral of desire itself creates a new pocket of time, complete with new tenses and verbal modes such as the conditionals, optatives, and subjunctives, within which new kinds of magic, and a dense new interplay of information— the poetry of life—can emerge. When Prospero draws aside the curtain of his cell to reveal the young lovers, they are not making, as they might have been making, the beast with two backs. They are playing chess, which is a world itself of interpersonal complexity, one in which the natural physical strength of the male is cancelled and compulsion thus irrelevant; one in which one can cheat without wickedness, and be intimate without collapsing the delicate structure and dignity of personhood. Of course in marriage the miracle is accomplished, and we can be both beast and spirit; but we must first learn to be spirit and not beast. To learn how to make the game of life real, we must first learn how to make reality into a game.

The chess game was so compelling a symbol that Bergman found he had to borrow it for his *Magic Flute*. He "discovers" Tamino and Pamina playing chess backstage during the intermission, adding another level to its meaning; art, acting, is also a game. The very borrowing of such an allusion is a gamelike anachronism, a way of short-circuiting time to make free space within which new things can happen.

In the course of the ordeals the Beast-Man is defeated, partly through the use of his own powers and friendlier aspects, partly through the use of technologies and magic talismans upon whose use the Wizard can advise but which were first provided by the Witch.

Finally the Witch herself is defeated by the Prince and Princess. (The defeat is literal in *Oz* and *Flute;* in *The Tempest* the figure of Venus in Prospero's masque substitutes for the absent Witch.) But now there is an amazing reversal. It turns out that a large part of the Wizard's power lies in the fiction or suasion of his legitimacy, and that he is weary of his task and eager to pass it on to the young initiates. He has been hoping that they would find the courage and maturity to unmask him, and takes the opportunity to unburden himself of his immortality and rejoin the human race. It is now time for the hero and heroine to maintain the beautiful fiction or game of reason, morality, and culture. Though they will know that it is indeed only a game, they will have learned through the experience of their ordeals and the battle with the Witch that it is a game worth the sacrifice of one's life.

Something further needs to be said about the magic talisman. Its deep ambiguity (Does it come from the Witch or the Wizard, or from some force prior to them? Is its power natural or a matter of convention and persuasion?) resembles that of talismans in other myths. These include the golden bough of Aeneas, the metatron of Moses, the lyre of Orpheus, and the caduceus of Hermes (which Hermes originally got from Apollo in exchange for the lyre—the lyre which Apollo in turn gave to his son Orpheus). Part of the ambiguity about the talisman's provenance comes from the necessarily protean character of a myth-device that must conduct its bearer across different spheres of being, often between the lands of the living and of the dead. In a sense the talisman is the very power of metaphor, the boundary-crossing significatory function, by which we understand and interpret the myth itself.

Prospero's talismanic book has, we assume, come with him into exile from his library in Milan. His talismanic staff is more problematic; possibly it is from the island. With their help he has made graves open and wake their sleepers (possibly in Shakespeare's previous play, *The Winter's Tale,* in which the playwright/Wizard brings the statue of a dead queen to life). At the end he breaks the staff and drowns the book, and dissolves their power, for they have served their moral function; and there is a strong impression that in a sense he is giving them *back* whence they came. Importantly, and unlike in the other versions of the myth, Prospero does not give the magic items to his daughter and son-in-law. The young people are provided with a profound moral training and great temporal power, but magic is not for them.

Why? For various reasons. One is that magic was still associated in Shakespeare's time with the black arts and, though acceptable in the magic island/theater, should not be imported into the "real world" of Milan and Naples. King James had banished them from *his* kingdom. Another reason is that true magic is actually technology based in sound science, as Shakespeare, through his acquaintance with such figures as the brilliant scientist Thomas Harriot, was coming to suspect. But such a technology did not yet exist, except in the field of theatrical illusion. Just as today we can make marvelous films of spaceships and galactic civilizations, but cannot yet mount a proper expedition to our nearest planetary neighbor, so their imaginative technology had run ahead of their physical capacity. Thus, when Prospero's play comes to an end, so must his magic. Interestingly enough, Prospero's magic cloak or mantle is not renounced, though he does change into normal clothing to meet his guests at the end. He can still *play* the Wizard; and perhaps such play is, in 1611, the only legitimate kind of magic. Any other kind is not intellectually justifiable; and if it were possible, can become compulsion and tyranny.

For perhaps, in 1611, we were not politically ready for magic. Prospero himself had lost his kingdom because of his magical studies; and one could imagine also his opposite, the tyrant who uses magic to compel a whole nation. If technology is effective magic, we could well argue that the great tyrants of our century did exactly that. Perhaps Shakespeare felt instinctively that one could not entrust such magic into the hands of an absolute ruler, and that we would have to wait for democracy, in which the powers would be distributed into the hands of the people and their danger neutralized, before it would be politically safe to offer such command over nature. (Considering our impact on the environment, is it safe even now?) It is not a coincidence that Shakespeare refers repeatedly to the New World in this play. In a mythic sense he is already preparing the intellectual soil for the United States of America, the regime of popular magic.

Most fundamentally of all, Prospero's decision to renounce the book and staff is not so much a negative rejection of magic as a positive choice of mortality. Like Odysseus on his magic island, Ogygia ("Noplace," or, in Latin, "Utopia"), Prospero chooses to go home and to die. And if his magic is

indeed powerful enough to raise the dead, he must get rid of
it. Death is too valuable an experience to forgo. Shakespeare
is anticipating a little problem that we shall be facing in a
hundred years or so: given the choice of physical immortality, how do we make meaning of our lives?

Here it might be objected that though Prospero can
fairly choose death for himself, yet in not giving the talismans to his children, he is depriving them of their choice of
immortality. Rather, I think, he recognizes that they themselves have, without being fully aware of it, already decided:
that the immortality of having children is more valuable
than the immortality of continued personal survival. They
are in love and can hardly wait to consummate their desires
in fertile sexual union. Prospero accepts their choice and
thus does not give them the gift of personal immortality.
And this somehow implies that immortality necessarily
comes packaged with sterility. Which, in turn, solves the
riddle of *A Midsummer Night's Dream:* Why should the
King and Queen of Fairyland be quarreling over the possession of a little mortal child? Because, being immortal, they
cannot have children themselves!

Biology itself presents us with the same mythic paradox.
There are two modes by which life propagates itself into the
future: one is by asexual reproduction—cloning—which pre-
serves the exact identity of the organism into the future, but
which is sterile in the sense that it does not produce unique
new offspring. An asexually reproducing organism is essentially immortal. The other is sexual reproduction, which
creates true individuals, but which always involves the
death of the parent (otherwise the adaptive advantage of
greater genetic variation, and swifter evolution, would be
lost). Sex goes with death. And if the cells of a sexually-
reproducing organism like ourselves should become immortal, and lose their programmed tendency to die after a
certain number of self-copyings, then they would be cancer

cells. Politically speaking, too, an immortal human being among mortals would be a cancer. All he or she would need to do would be to invest some money at compound interest, wait for a few hundred years, and buy the planet.

Prospero does not, in any case, annihilate the powers of the book and staff. He disperses them into the medium of the island and the sea; to the extent that the island and sea represent the tradition of the theater itself and the forces of creative dreaming, he, like Shakespeare himself at the end of his creative life, is simply re-liquefying the energies which he has temporarily held bound. He frees them, as he frees Ariel, for the use of other artists; and thus he is passing the talismans on after all, not to his literal offspring but to his artistic progeny.

Much of this excursion on the talismans of *The Tempest* applies also to *The Magic Flute* and *The Wizard of Oz*. In *Flute,* there is the same sense that the choice of progeny is the choice of mortality; and in *Oz,* Dorothy chooses to use the red slippers to renounce an immortal fairyhood for the sake of a real life (and death) in Kansas. Some minor differences exist between the earlier version of the myth and the two later ones. In *The Tempest* no explicit talisman symbolizes the gifts of Sycorax and Caliban; instead, there is Ariel (who is controlled by the book and staff, but not created by them), and Caliban's knack for knowing the brine pits and fresh springs, and possibly Miranda's budding sexuality.

In the latter two versions of the myth at least some of the talismanic gifts come from the Witch, and a more or less clear distinction exists between the gifts of the Wizard and those of the Witch. The bells of Papageno (in Bergman's version, painted with a little eighteenth-century erotic scene) are given to him by the Queen of Night. She also gives Tamino the flute, but it seems that the flute was first found by Sarastro in an oak tree. Dorothy's red shoes, as we have seen, definitely come from the Witch. But the Doctorate of

Thinkology, the Medal of Valor, and the Testimonial of Beneficence, by which the Straw Man, the Lion, and the Tin Man achieve their desires, are given by the Wizard, and their nature is interestingly different.

These gifts from the Wizard are performative in nature, that is, they make their statement true by the utterance of it. They add to, or graft onto, nature a second nature while at the same time confirming as a fact what was previously held as an intention. By means of these gifts, the Wizard, as Gonzalo puts it in *The Tempest,* arranges for all of us to find ourselves, "when no man was his own." If the gifts of the Witch symbolize our natural inheritance—including aesthetic aptitudes like Caliban's love of music and Papageno's Orphic use of the bells to quell the forces of nature—then the gifts of the Wizard symbolize the new performative powers of reason, imagination, and will which are mutated out of that natural inheritance. The flute seems to combine both nature and culture, like a fully mature artistic talent, in a natural-classical union. The talismans also illustrate the evolution of natural biological technology into a newer, faster, and more intentionally controllable cultural technology.

The last major ingredient of the myth is the magic land itself. It is a land of wonder, and wonder is the central emotion of the whole myth; indeed wonder is enjoined on us as the most appropriate response to the world, to our existence, and to each other. "O wonder," says Miranda (whose name means wonder); O brave new world. Finally, that is the wisest thing we can say about it. Dr. Marvel's name means the same thing. And the music of *The Magic Flute* is a triumphant combination of Mozart's great themes of forgiveness, excited urgency at the approach of death, and delighted wonder. The magic land is as as bright and fresh as a dream, as a rainbow; both dream and rainbow are part of its imagery. It is in brilliant Technicolor, where ordinary life is in shades of gray. The best description of it is in Prospero's masque, with its turfy mountains, its nibbling sheep, its crisp brooks, unshrubbed down and bosky acres, and its blue rainbow. It is an arcadian and pastoral place, cut off or islanded from the real world.

In the magic island different versions of reality can be tried out. As a land of dream it represents the alternative psychological spaces of the person, not bound by the convention of a single awake rational self. A political playground, it can serve as a *Gedankenexperiment*—a thought-experiment—where various utopias can be tried out, including Gonzalo's naturalistic anarchy, Prospero's and Sarastro's magical philosopher kingdoms, bucolic democratic Munchkinland and populist/urban/technocratic/Tammany/bossist Emerald City. As an artistic space, the island is itself a theater, a picture frame, a field of musical thematic motifs. In another sense, it is a sort of Disneyland, carnival, or circus. As in Aristophanes' Cloudcuckooland we are on holiday there and do not need to take things too seriously; though what we do there is the most serious thing in our lives, to find out the meaning of life. It is a test-bed, limbec, or laboratory for new ideas, alchemical, psychological, social, scientific, and philosophical.

The magic land is also a fairyland, that is, a place intermediate in nature between Heaven and Hell. According to an old legend the fairies were originally angels neutral in the war between the hosts of Satan and St. Michael, who were cast out of Heaven when Satan was defeated; they did not fall all the way to Hell but settled in the middle air about the Earth, and offer a third way to the human seeker. When, in the ballad, Thomas the Rhymer sees a beautiful lady on a horse by the crossroads of the Eildon Tree, he asks her if she is the queen of Heaven. She replies that she is not, but that she is the queen of Fairyland, and that, if he kisses her, she will possess his body. Of course, he does kiss her; she makes him get up on the horse behind her, and they ride off through strange lands until they come to a place where three ways lead off from their path. One is the broad and easy path down to Hell; one is the steep and rocky path up to Heaven; but the third, which they take, is a bonny path that winds about the ferny brae. It is the road to fair Elfland. That open-ended, helically winding, evolutionary third path, distinct from the dead ends of Heaven and Hell, is the way of the Yellow Brick Road, the way that the Wizard points out to the Prince and Princess, and is the future of the human race. The story of Thomas is perhaps the story of how the Wizard got to be the Wizard: Thomas's reward is that he will become a poet and speaker of the truth.

In another sense yet the magic land is a paradise—which is what Ferdinand calls it—and is thus both the land of the ever-living and the land of the dead. The implication is that it is a place where we cannot stay; we must leave it, as Prospero and his friends must leave the island and as Dr. Marvel and Dorothy must leave Oz, and return to real life. We discover the open-endedness of the world in Oz but, in order to pursue it, must return to Earth, where death is still to come. In *The Magic Flute* the return to earth is only implied, not stated; the audience must leave the theater and go home.

The topology of the magic island is rather peculiar, and until the recent discovery of fractal geometry there existed no way of clearly describing it. It exists in the world, but is cut off from it by a finite boundary, often spherical or circular. ("The great globe itself" is Prospero's term, punning between the planet Earth and the Globe Theater, which would indeed "dissolve," as Prospero prophesied, in a fire two years after the first performance of *The Tempest.*) The dome of the just pagans in Dante's *Inferno,* bounded on the outside but spacious and lit by its own light on the inside, is a precursor of this place. The cave of the dragon-men in Blake's memorable fancy of the printing-house in Hell is another version.

Within the dome of the magic land there is an infinite

inner space, much like Koch curves, the space-filling arabesques of Peano or the infinitely recursive patterns of the Mandelbrot Set. The Yellow Brick Road, with its initiatory spiral, is a diagram of that endless space; so also is the generativeness of Mozart's thematic material in the music of the opera. The magic island is thus a symbol of a putative human capacity to create or discover a "paradise within thee, happier far," as Milton puts it, unlimited by our external constraints of space, time, and death, an informational universe that is boundlessly deep and generative, and which resists and reverses the tendency of the world to decay and run down.

Finally, the magic land is an Eden, that is, a place where the fundamental mythic rules were written, and where, perhaps, they can be rewritten. The myth itself is the rewriting of those rules: and here we may begin an exegesis of the myth as a whole.

The new myth imagines a humanity that is at last grown up; is no longer newborn, like Adam and Eve, or adolescent, like Prometheus. The Wizard is at least as wise as the Jehovah of the Old Testament; perhaps wiser, because he has had the experience of checks and reverses, has a sense of humor, and is going to choose mortality over immortality, an experience of choice forbidden to deities. The setting is an Eden, but not the original one, where all the trouble started—trouble largely caused by the expectation that there should be no trouble. In the new myth, trouble is the dynamo of history. The old age of the Wizard symbolizes the maturity of the human race; the young protagonists, its hope for the future. Perhaps the proper time of the myth will never come, when we have human mages capable of negotiating a new contract for the species, and thus perhaps the myth will always be properly a myth of the future; but a myth of the future might be a useful thing to have, and a source of esperance and even prosperity.

That new contract will be one in which we are freer; more realistic; less prone to illusion and false hope; less in need of psychological distortions such as guilt, internalized fear of retribution, and infantile dependence to keep us moral; more empowered scientifically and technologically; more creative; and more in harmony with the rest of nature and with our own nature.

The myth is of special interest to America. Prospero's magic island closely resembles the Bermuda (the "still-vex'd Bermoothes") of the wrecked but miraculously rescued second Virginia expedition, and Oz can be found over any Kansas rainbow. *The Magic Flute* was first performed in Vienna in 1791, the date of the ratification of the U.S. Bill of Rights. The political identity of America, whether or not it lives up to it, is bound up in the possibility of a new Edenic contract. The future of the myth, I have no doubt, is closely linked to the exploration of outer space, the creation of satellite garden-worlds in orbit round the Earth and Sun, and the terraforming and colonization of the planets Mars and Venus.

Let us contrast the provisions of the new deal for human beings that is being worked out in the magic island with those of the old deal, as it is well expressed in the Book of Genesis. Much of the meaning of the new contract can be summarized by listing which of the ancient roles, prohibitions, permissions, duties, taboos, curses, and blessings of humankind are now associated with the prelapsarian state, and which with the fallen state.

First of all, significantly, the mage himself has replaced Jehovah as father-figure. He is an amateur Jehovah, and both knows and admits it; and he will shed the role as soon as ever he can. The role of parent is radically changed. In the old myth the parent retains the full parental authority throughout the lifetime of the child; in the new myth the very raison d'être of the parent is to prepare the child for freedom from parental authority, so that the child can in turn be an effective parent. If God is our father, the new myth says, then he should do what any good father does, which is to bring up his child to the point where he or she no longer has any need of a parent or superordinate authority. God's true work is to abolish our need for God.

The Fall (the return to real life from the island) is seen in the new dispensation as a natural and desirable development, rather than as a disaster. The disobedience that results in the Fall is now seen as virtuous and is actively encouraged by the Wizard.

In the old Eden, sexual activity was permitted freely, happily, and polymorphously (if without fertility) before the Fall, but is hedged about with guilt, grief, and misfortune after it. The two contracts are similar in placing sexual *reproduction* after the Fall (in Genesis we reproduce asexually by fission, like an amoeba, before the Fall: Eve is born parthenogenetically out of Adam's side). In the old myth, childbirth after the Fall will be painful and miserable; but, in the new myth, it will be a source of delight. In the new myth, sex is one of the rewards for a successful Fall, whereas in the old the partial withdrawal of sex is one of the punishments for the Fall.

In other words, the new myth is more severe in its sexual morality than the old: Ferdinand and Miranda, and Tamino and Pamina, are forbidden sexual contact before the Fall, whereas Adam and Eve were permitted it. Thus, the myth is much more revolutionary than the conventional modernistic doctrine of sexual license, which falls into the trap and offers the role of the naughty child provided by the old myth. In the Old Testament, sex after the Fall is fraught with evils. However, in the new myth, sex after the Fall is good, fertile, delightful, and unguilty, though entirely within the context of marriage, that is, human choice and spiritual freedom. (Sexual uncontrol would presumably throw us back to the unfree world of unilateral or mutual rape, associated with the Beast-Man, the Witch, and the Dragon.)

Marriage is of central importance in the new myth. Many of the tests that the young heroine and hero must undergo are trials of the virtues specifically required for a successful marriage: commitment, friendship, tolerance, equality, faithfulness, respect, continence, patience, and fortitude. Where marriage is, in the old myth, a sort of sea-anchor to limit the moral damage caused by our disordered and fallen nature, in the new myth it is an initiation into wizardhood, even into the kind of limited, mortal, and amateur deity to which human nature can now aspire. Marriage is a celebration and symbol of the new phase of evolution that we will have reached in the future epoch that the myth describes.

In the old myth, sexual inequality essentially begins after the Fall and is one of the evils it brings. In the new myth, sexual inequality is abolished by the Fall: the male Wizard will pass on his power equally to his daughter and son-in-law, or even, in the case of Oz, to the "daughter" alone.

In the old myth, Adam and Eve lived in a state of blissful and untedious leisure; work was one of the evils attendant upon the Fall. In the new myth, Ferdinand must pile up logs and Miranda volunteers to help him; Tamino, Pamina, Papageno, Dorothy and her helpers must endure exhausting quests, ordeals, and tasks before they are permitted the honor of the Fall. Fall becomes a sort of graduation, the conferral of the Th.D. Not that they can now relax after their achievement: their trials are but qualifications for a whole lifetime of productive endeavor. Thus, work is given a positive meaning, and is subtly changed from being identified with labor and punishment to being identified with education and creation.

The new myth is essentially evolutionary in its cosmology. It represents a third position between the traditional religious dogma of creation, in which the world of nature and of our own nature is a sort of layout or diorama into which human souls have been placed, and the opposite but corresponding modernist notion in which the world is a passive and protean material to be shaped by human will. In the new myth, nature evolves through its own process of self-transcendence, and its history and achieved order must be known through science if anything is to be achieved; but we human beings are increasingly charged with the responsibility of guiding and embodying that process.

The myth gives several stages of human development, from the primitive forces of the tempest, whirlwind, and Dragon, through the mammalian compulsions of the Witch and the ungoverned vitality of the Beast-Man, to the noble young initiates and the wizardhood into which they are now inducted. The tests themselves are a kind of education in evolutionary ethics and science; the young hero and heroine must recapitulate the long struggle by which we achieved our humanity. They must, like the heroes, poets, and spiritual voyagers of epic, go down into the underworld of the evolutionary past, analyze their mature humanity into its moral primitives, and in the arduous course of their return to the light, recreate from that underworld their own new synthesis.

One of the chief hazards in their pilgrimage is the threat of addiction. Civilization's ultimate measure is the strength of the drugs, narcotics, and intoxicants it can override and thus withstand. When we set out to retrace our passage to full humanity, we must in a sense divest ourselves of some of our normal supports—our habits and routines, the pressure of custom, the rule of normalcy. We're not in Kansas anymore. Only in this way can we be open to the feeling of wonder that is the central emotive lesson of the myth. In this naked state, we are easy prey for those chemistries which interfere with the lower, involuntary levels of brain processing. Thus, our examples of the myth include the drunkenness of Stephano and Trinculo, Caliban's susceptibility to control through alcohol addiction, the general addictive appetitiveness of Papageno, the paralyzing of Monostatos' followers by the sweetness of the bells, and of course the beautiful red field of opium poppies in *The Wizard of Oz* which sends all the questers but for the faithful but helpless machine-man to sleep.

In the *Odyssey*, Odysseus and his followers must withstand similar temptations, and Polyphemus the Beast-Man is overcome by the hero's strong civilized wine; Enkidu in *Gilgamesh* is domesticated by means of such addictions, and Adam and Eve in Milton's *Paradise Lost* go on a toot after their Fall. The difference between the old myth and the new is subtle at this point. In the old myth, addiction is equated with pleasure in general, and although it is an evil, it is useful as a way of trapping the free energies of human beings into the servility of society. In the new myth, addiction is distinguished from pleasure: part of the test is to be able to separate the redness of the poppies from the redness of Dorothy's magic slippers, the grand liquor of Stephano from the delight of Prospero's masque, the astonishing beauty of the Queen of Night's vengeful arias from that of the hymns of Sarastro.

The evolution of these powers of discrimination involves the origins of language. In the old myth, language is simply given to human beings as part of the soul breathed into them by the Creator. It is designed to tell the truth, and the Fall consists partly in the first lies that the ur-children tell to their ur-parent. There is no distinction between lies and fictions, and indeed fiction, games, and acknowledged pretense have no place in the old myth. The new myth regards human language as an emergent property of nature, prepared for by our prior evolution, and as fictional in its very essence (though fiction, as we shall see, has real ontological effects). Caliban is taught to speak by Prospero, but though he can recognize the organic and sensory traces of beauty, and his own language sometimes has the natural beauty of an animal's song, he cannot appreciate fictions and poetry and uses language chiefly for cursing. All Caliban can do is tell the truth. As we have seen, his inability to appreciate fictions puts him at an advantage over the more degraded products of civilization, like Stephano and Trinculo; he sees through the finery with which Prospero baits the hook to catch the conspirators. The emperor, for Caliban, never has any clothes.

But the meaning of the new myth is that the emperor's imaginary clothes can have the most profound spiritual significance. Prospero's masque of spirits is just a pastime, in one sense—a delightful show to distract the lovers from their passionate desires. But in another sense it is a symbol of that delay between desire and fulfilment, initial conditions and final heat-death, debt and payment, which holds open our brief window of time between the two eternities that lie before the origin and after the end of the world. If the sexual and mortal debt is paid off at once, then life ceases; life, and its intensification in consciousness, is a sort of postponing, a litigation, an equivocation, a staving-off by interest payments, of the day of reckoning. As Prigogine and others have shown, nature is full of such delaying games, which so complicate the determinate fall of the universe toward final stasis that an infinite but bounded fractal hierarchy can emerge within the temporal space which is opened up.

We do not need an eternal lawgiver to be moral; all we need is a fiction-making power that is itself as deeply good in its aim and wise in its application as the old Divine Father was. In *King Lear* it becomes clear that there is no divine providence in charge of things, and the death of Cordelia at the very end of the play, in plain contradiction to the sources of Shakespeare's story, hammers that fact home. But there is no rule that says we cannot *pretend* that there is a divine mercy and justice, and act as if they were real, even if we know they are only "make-believe."

Edgar, in disguise as the madman Tom, tricks his blind and despairing father Gloster into believing that he has leaped from the cliffs of Dover and has been miraculously saved by the merciful gods. It is a marvelous piece of stage bravura—it would be hard for an audience to tell whether Gloster's fall is a theatrical mime of a real fall or a theatrical mime of a fall as harmless as the one the actor takes on stage. The audience itself is drawn into a beautiful fiction, no less real for being fictional, of redemption and salvation. And Gloster is really saved, and comes to believe in the real truth that his "life's a miracle," through the masque of his rescue from death. Later, Edgar will appear in the armor of St. Michael the archangel, heralded by three archangelic blasts of the trumpet, to confront his evil brother Edmund and stage a provisional version of the Last Judgment. By putting on the clothing of a moral emperor, and playing the part to the hilt, we make a moral realm come into being.

By fiction, then, and by poetry, we can performatively create a paradise of love and justice. When we do so, we are continuing the evolutionary work of nature itself. Part of our work is to understand and recapitulate where we came from; Edgar must be prepared for his role by living the life of the Beast-Man, Poor Tom. Only thus, paradoxically, can we create a new world. Thus, the scientific, or truth-telling, function of language cannot be detached from its poetic, or fiction-making function. And the possibility of lies is the risk we take.

As in *The Tempest,* so also in *Flute* and *Oz,* the fiction-making power of language can be misused to tell lies. The more primitive levels of nature distrust such powers. Papageno's lies are silenced not by Sarastro but by the ladies of the Queen of Night. Fiction is nevertheless one of the emergent gifts of a higher morality. The emergence of language is the emergence of a new stage of meta-evolution. Its miraculous capacity for feedback, reflexivity, self-inclusion and thus self-transcendence is central to both the medium and the meaning of the new myth.

It might appear at this point that the new myth is altogether more optimistic and perhaps unrealistic than the old. The assumption that human beings may become wise enough to govern themselves morally without an external divine sanction is perhaps a doubtful one: Can we trust mere human beings to make the rules? One might reply that human lawmakers who do not believe they have the sanction and backing of God are a good deal less dangerous than those who believe they have God on their side. And should we abandon the quest for human wisdom because of its difficulty?

There is one major theme, moreover, on which the new myth has much less of comfort to say than the old: that is, death. All three versions of the new myth seem to accept the unavoidability and finality of death; the old myth, however, sees death as not natural to human beings and as a punishment for the sin of disobedience. A punishment can be rescinded by the punisher; and thus the old myth, even without its later expansion into doctrines of the afterlife, holds out a kind of hope. But that escape which promises continued personal existence after the grave seems to be closed or at least unnecessary in the new dispensation. Indeed, by Prospero's art, graves have waked their sleepers and sent them forth; but these resurrections were theatrical fictions, like the revival of Hermione in *The Winter's Tale,* and signified the extraordinary miracle of rebirth that can happen in a person's life. The sculptor of Hermione's statue, which is to come to life, significantly presents her wrinkled and silvered, as she might have aged during the period since her "death." There is no escape from time. Time is the only medium of reality, and time means death.

But having accepted death, we paradoxically become free of it. This is a great mystery, beyond ordinary consolation, for it denies nothing to tragedy. The chief test of Tamino and Pamina is silence, which signifies precisely the silence of the wise on this issue, and their ability to become one, and thus in a way immortal, by facing the irrevocability of death together. Like Odysseus, Dorothy chooses to go back to the mortal world where her life is in imminent danger; as his from old age, so hers from the fever brought on by her illness. They identify themselves in solidarity with loved mortals—Penelope, Aunt Em. Prospero's every third thought will be of the grave. And this choice of death is a necessary part of that new mythic package which comes with so many hopeful and happy gifts.

The new myth is also much less comfortable than the old in its doctrine of the nature of the soul. In the old myth, the soul is conferred by divine power, breathed into our inert bodies as a spark of God's own essence. This is a beautiful idea; but it carries with it the implication that if we sin we deserve to be damned in the flames of Hell forever: a spark of God has no excuses. The corollary to this myth is that if we are to have compassion on human weakness, we had better give up the existence of the soul altogether, and treat human beings either as irresponsible animals or as the resultants of socioeconomic forces. Once the old myth relaxed its grip, the West did indeed tend to collapse and bifurcate into one of these two positions, both implicit in the old myth though denied by it. The first of these two alternatives to the existence of the soul resulted in Nazism, national socialism, wherein a person's value derived from his or her race. The second resulted in Communism, wherein our identity is based on social class. Both were bloody monstrosities. We need the idea of the soul.

The new myth contains the interesting suggestion that the soul is real but synthetic, created in an evolutionary process by other persons and by itself out of the raw materials of its heredity and cultural environment. Thus, it is possible for a person never to develop a truly free and original soul; but the myth goes on to propose that it is precisely those biological or social automata to whom the souled owe the greatest debt of charity, because in a sense they are innocent. Prospero is strangely merciful to the unrepentant and cynical traitors Antonio and Sebastian, and forgives them, "unnatural though thou art," despite the fact that they show no sign of changing their ideas. He is content that his knowledge of their misdeeds is sufficient to keep them in line in the future, and knows that, as socioeconomically-determined beings and as beings determined to be socioeconomically determined, they will never change. Essentially, as believers in the supremacy of political power, they will never develop proper souls and therefore should not be held responsible for moral and spiritual matters of which they are incapable. Thus, the myth would advise us not to hold economic reductionists of the right and left responsible for their actions, as we might a genuine moral agent, but to find gentle ways of knowledge to hold them in check and protect their neighbors from them.

Prospero also forgives Caliban, Shakespeare's illustration of what a noble savage might really be like, if there could be such a thing. (Part of his meaning is that there could not be such an animal.) Caliban is a biologically-determined being, "upon whose nature nurture will never stick." He too cannot be held responsible for a soul, though he certainly has more of one than the Marxist/Capitalist conspirators. Prospero even rewards Caliban for his betrayal by bequeathing the island to him when he leaves. Sarastro and his followers similarly give Papageno an easy ride when he flunks his tests. Of course, it would not be fair to say that

Papageno has no soul, but it is an embryonic or infantile one. On the other hand, in *The Wizard of Oz,* the Scarecrow, Tin Man, and Cowardly Lion begin as artificial or biological automata but achieve their souls in the course of their service to Dorothy, showing a more optimistic American slant to the myth. But to compensate, as it were, the Witch receives much harsher treatment than in the other versions.

The developed soul cannot be found either in nature or in nurture alone. But in some people a complex feedback process, between a nature that is already partly social and a culture which incorporates a wisdom about human nature, has made possible the emergence of a unique self-ordering and self-determining entity that fulfills the classical definitions of a soul. Education is essential to this mysterious kindling, this moment when seeming chaos begins reflexively to generate its own order, its own entelechy, its own strange attractors. The educations of Miranda, Ferdinand, Tamino, Pamina, and Dorothy are at the heart of the myth, and their ordeals are what Keats called the "vale of soul-making."

The new myth avoids the twin traps of the fallenness and the perfectibility of the soul, since it does not set up the soul as an apriori essence which might be inspected to reveal criteria of perfection. Each new soul is a unique achievement, like a work of art; with the unpredictability yet inevitability-after-the-fact that is the hallmark of good art. Since death is final, there is no retribution beyond the grave. The soul is conferred performatively upon us by each other, by our love and imagination and prayer and invocation of it; and by ourselves, by our choice of self-discipline, our habits of love, service, honesty, and self-knowledge.

We must even confer the honor and prerogatives of a soul upon those human beings in whom the kindling never took place, whether as a result of genetic damage or a cultural and family background so brutal that it was snuffed out—or, more tragically, through a chosen miseducation in cynicism and reductionism. Sometimes, if we treat someone as if they had a free and responsible soul, they come to possess one; and to be able to assist in the birth of a soul would surely be the highest of achievements. It is in the sharedness of soul-making, the involvement of others in the conferral and recognition of the soul, that such immortality as we possess resides. We finally are only what we give away, only what no longer has any taint of possession about it. What lasts is exactly what can be fully experienced by others as themselves!

Though the soul, in the new myth, is not an apriori essence and cannot therefore be examined for what would perfect it, values are not impossible. We honestly can and do recognize goodness, beauty, and truth in persons and things, though indeed the recognition process is itself much more like the forming of a strange attractor than like the application of a set of principles. And that recognition is largely shared. Most arguments for the arbitrariness of value, cultural relativism and subjectivism, on examination, turn out to be based on anecdotes of personal and social value-differences, such as the differences in artistic taste between two people, or different food taboos or marriage-customs in various parts of the world. But these anecdotes can only be stated and only make sense as examples if writer and reader share a gigantic pre-interpreted database and an enormous stock of agreed values. Without these, as cognitive science is making very clear, no communication would be possible at all. Human and animal ethology, the comparative study of ritual and myth, and new work on aesthetic and artistic universals confirm that this consensus extends across all of humankind, and its roots go back to the animal kingdom. The education of the Prince and Princess is an education in those recognitions.

But is not the new knowledge that they learn, and that

we learn through the telling of the myth, a forbidden knowledge? Our three versions have about them a taint of proscribed magic, which is disguised by their playfulness and lightness of tone. Even so, *The Wizard of Oz* was on the list of banned works put out by a fundamentalist group intent on protecting school children from dangerous ideas. They were right in banning it, for it is deeply subversive to their position, which is that we are divinely-operated automata; not self-made, and mutually-made, free souls. Indeed, if the proponents of such naturalistic positions as Deep Ecology had the insight to see it, they should ban it too, for it insists that it is natural for us to change Nature.

But let us take these objections seriously. To what extent is the whole enterprise of the myth a blasphemous and sacrilegious tampering with God's, or Nature's, arrangement of things? The myth answers that it isn't, because the whole story is unserious anyway, a fiction, a game, set off from the real world in Never-Never Land, Oz, Cloudcuckooland. So God (and Mother Nature) can't object to it, as we are not asserting it, but only pretending, making-believe. But suppose it were a better arrangement than God's original plan?—and suppose God is really like Prospero and Sarastro and Dr. Marvel, and he secretly *wants* us to renegotiate our contract? Has he in fact been waiting for us to do it all this time, and wondering why we were taking so long, considering how rebellious, how contrary, how like himself he had made us? What if he were even a little disappointed in us, a little tired of running the universe all by himself, and was waiting for us to grow up? Or what if it were Mother Nature, the Good Witch, who is waiting for us to put our magic red slippers to work?

But will human nature permit the new world to be created? Or can human nature actually assist in the work? We are, after all, animals. Does the new dispensation demand too much of us? We need the aggressiveness of the Lion, the cheerfulness of Papageno, the instinct for fertility and the natural wisdom of Caliban. But they are not enough, and must be disciplined to be made productive. We have to rely on innate capacities we have, for civilization, self-control, goodness, service, and self-sacrifice, exemplified by Miranda, Ferdinand, Pamina, Tamino, and Dorothy. For the authors of these versions of the myth, the sources of such innate capacities were mysterious and unreliable, and there was no rational explanation of whence they originated. We are now beginning to find out that the overlap between biological and cultural evolution provided us with genes for those essential qualities, genes which are expressed in just enough people to make a humane and creative society possible, perhaps, if we have the right kind of political structure and technology. So we are in a unique position at the beginning of a new millennium to put the beautiful myth into effect.

We stand at the frontier of the solar system and the galaxy. We need a new dispensation now, for the magic islands we shall plant out there in the great ocean of space. We can look to these eloquent and charming stories for guidance in our efforts. Oz lies up there among the stars.

# LIFE ON MARS: CULTIVATING A PLANET— AND OURSELVES

MARS IS ONE OF THE BRIGHTEST OB-
jects in the night sky. Its reddish color, now
known to be caused by the prevalence of
iron oxides in its soil, perhaps accounts for
its identification by the Greeks and Ro-
mans with the bloody god of war. Its astronomical symbol is the same as the circle-and-arrow symbol
of the male and of the metal iron. Like all planets—"wanderers"—it does not make an orderly circuit of Polaris, as do
the fixed stars, but pursues an odd, looping trajectory
through the sky, and waxes and wanes in brightness as it
does so. The orderly astronomical mind, intrigued by this
irregularity in the orbits of planets, arrived after some ten
thousand years of speculation at the present model of the
solar system, wherein Mars circles the sun in the same plane

as Earth, but at about one-third again the distance away (about 228 million kilometers). From Mars, the sun would look about two thirds of the size it looks from here. Mars is smaller than Earth, and its surface gravitation is about three eighths of Earth's. Its year—the period in which it revolves about the sun—is about twice as long as an Earth year, but the inclination of its poles is almost identical to Earth's, and thus its seasonal variations are analogous: it has a spring, a summer, an autumn, and a winter. Its day—the period in which it spins on its own axis—is almost exactly identical to Earth's.

We have always projected upon the stars the images of our own archetypes, and Mars has been a rich field for such imaginative colonization. Indeed, the twentieth-century mythology of the planet is perhaps richer than at any prior period. The eyes of the astronomers Lowell and Schiaparelli, straining against the distortion of Earth's atmosphere as they peered through their telescopes, interpreted the orange blur into a surface webbed with lines. The planet of canals they hypothesized became in turn the evocative basis of the Mars many of us grew up with: the Mars of the great deserts, the dying planet of Edgar Rice Burroughs and H. G. Wells, with its thin air, its ancient despairing civilizations eking out the last precious water from the melting poles, its envious glances at the blue water-planet between them and the sun. In the extraordinary panic that followed Orson Welles' radio dramatization of *The War of the Worlds,* Mars became the great American symbol of The Other—ancient where we were young, in want where we were surrounded by natural fertility, subtle and incalculable where we were simple: like the Europeans, perhaps, or the Orientals, or, in Burroughs' fantasy, like the North American Indians we had dispossessed and driven into the deserts.

Nevertheless, we yearned for there to be life on Mars, and the evidence for a while looked good: Mars clearly had an atmosphere, and weather, and changed color at different times of the year. For these and other reasons Mars became a major focus of NASA's planetary exploration program, and their efforts were rewarded by the spectacular success of the Mariner and Viking probes, which photographed, landed on, and sampled the Martian surface. But the result was bitter disappointment; Mars was biologically dead, and our almost religious hope for a sister species in the depths of space was deferred. On the level of cultural myth, many people turned inward, back to the precious and beautiful island of Earth and to the inner realm of personal experience, and abandoned the impulse of exploration. But that retreat also perhaps carried with it an ungenerous, timid and querulous element, a miserly hoarding of the spirit, which has permeated our economy, our educational system, and our arts. The Martians have perhaps done us more harm by their nonexistence than by their imagined invasion of our world.

But let us imagine another myth instead. In one of Ray Bradbury's stories an Earthly colonist of Mars takes his daughter down to the canal to show her a Martian. She is told to look into the water, and there she sees her own reflections. Suppose *we* were the Martians? Suppose we could go there and make the place our own? "We" in this case cannot, we know now, mean just we human beings. If the ecology movement has taught us anything, it is that we cannot exist without a biosphere of other species about us—they *are* us, are our bodies. So the new myth of Mars must be that we will bring Mars to life, and garden it into a place where the living descendants of Earthly plants and animals can flourish—a new nature, a new birth of a world into sentient existence.

But what would be the purpose of this enterprise? What would justify its enormous expense and danger? There are two answers to this question: one practical and economic (though based, as is all economics, on the mysterious sources of desire); the other philosophical or even pre-philosophical,

since it concerns a fundamental tuning of the mind that is
the prerequisite of true philosophy.

Economics first. We live in a time when despite the achievement of great wealth for huge continental populations in
many developed nations, there is a widespread sense of the
loss of value, meaning, dignity, and grandeur in our vision
of ourselves and our cosmos. We need the moral equivalent
of a great war or a great religion; or we will find it in drug
addiction, madness, and perhaps uncontrollable internal political violence. The young especially need to find in the
world an enterprise worth the life and death commitment of
a full, undamaged, uncynical, adult human being. The existence of such an enterprise would create a general improvement in morale as the peoples of the world realize that they
are working for something worthy of human attention, not
just for personal wealth or national prestige or out of the
exacerbated grievance that is the core of the Marxist/Capi-
talist theory of value.

One of the strangest things about human beings is that
we tend to achieve the most obviously desirable things only
when we are striving for something else. We are happiest
when we are striving not for happiness but, say, for artistic
perfection, or for the purest service to other persons, or for
true knowledge. Economically, the widespread well-being of
the great masses of people in Europe and America was not
achieved by any ambition to improve the lives of the poor—
in fact, it may have been hindered by it—but rather through
the pursuit of trade, exploration, art, religious evangelism,
science, and profit. The most stable and perhaps the most
contented society in the world has probably been ancient
Egypt, which for millenia poured all its surplus wealth
straight into the ground, in the form of gravegoods, tombs,
monuments, and pyramids. Death was its sink of excess
value. The contemporary stability of the world's economic

system—not in absolute terms, of course, but compared with all other periods of history—may well have a great deal to do with our own egregious and pyramidical form of waste, the arms race. With peace imminent between the East and the West, we are going to have to look very seriously for some commensurable and magnificent folly to keep the world economy going. It will be hard work spending the trillion or so annual dollars that presently find their home in the world's defense budget. The best candidate for the job is the Mars terraforming project.

The enormous expense of the project, then, is one of its great advantages; we are going to need something to replace the necessary economic waste of the arms race when nobody takes the threat of nuclear war seriously anymore. And to what better purpose might we put the beautiful and terrible heroic spirit of humankind, ready for suffering and sacrifice and courage, when we no longer have war to spend it on? There is in this proposal a strange continuity of technology and passion with the old art of war, combined with a reversal of purpose. The seeding process might put to appropriate use our huge stocks of ballistic missiles, replacing their warheads with the germs of life. Old clichés are sometimes very rich: this would indeed be a beating of swords into plowshares.

The flow of economic value, especially into the tropical areas that house the great preponderance of species on Earth, would be a significant tonic to the world's economy. Some have already suggested that the World Bank could trade forgiveness of Third World indebtedness for protection of the rain forests; in the light of the Mars project, and with a new juriprudence in which genes can be patented, the genetic information preserved in the forests would become a precious, salable, and renewable resource.

Meanwhile, the economic fallout from the new biotechnology should produce great new forms of wealth. The terraforming of Mars will require the complete recreation by human science, art, and technology of the natural ecology itself, and the creative extension of that ecology into new domains. We will be preparing ourselves to become the pollinators and the seeders of the universe, and to carry life not only to other planets in the solar system but also across the galaxy and to other galaxies. This project will require that we come to understand the molecular structure of life so well that we can reproduce existing life-forms, resurrect extinct forms, beneficially alter existing forms for new environments, and create entirely new kinds of life. Only thus could the hostile and sterile environments that lie beyond the blue mantle of Earth be seeded and gardened. In the process of this work we will discover how valuable is every single existing species, and perhaps even roll back the wave of extinctions that we have caused, by restoring lost species.

Who knows what new technologies might arise out of this effort? Why might we not here on Earth eventually live in houses grown from genetically-tailored trees? And mine our raw materials with the aid of multitudes of tiny bacterial or nanotechnological assistants programmed to strain the precious elements out of the sea or the ground, or extract them from our own waste-products? This increase in wealth, moreover, would not be at the expense of the $CO_2$ balance of the planet, nor would it generate pollution.

The world not being exclusively a linear and rational system, we may not be able to achieve all our immediately desirable objectives by striving for them. An excellent and universal education, which is our greatest need, may not be achievable merely by the direct application of resources and intentions to that purpose. Nor may, in the long run, any reversal of the process of environmental deterioration. Nor may any improvement in the condition of the world's poor, as we know from the Sahel and the American ghetto, where the aid and good intentions of one generation were largely responsible for the famines and the cultural collapse of the next. Of course, for our own moral sanity, we must do everything we can. But the real help will come from some other direction; it will be some incaluclable and autonomous movement of the human spirit, and will have to do, I believe, with the health of the stock of value in the world, its growth, its hope in itself.

So our deepest work must be like that of an artist, who by indirect means must make some beautiful richness flower up, who must nourish the ground of her art with strange conceptions. The Mars terraforming project is a "pyramid" whose building will force us to educate ourselves as we need to be educated, but behind our backs, while we are not, so to speak, looking. It will be at first a magnificent waste, which will prune our economic system to its most productive. Only later will we realize that it was in our economic interest, indeed was the key to our economic survival. This is the way the story of history happens—what was a game turns into our surest and soundest resource. This project will give birth to social, spiritual, and economic turbulences that will raise up the unfortunate, and cause us to seek out that knowledge and power by which we will save the environment from ourselves.

The second reason for undertaking the gardening of Mars is that it will be an essential part of our philosophical education as a species: an education that we desperately need. At present, the constructive energies of our culture are locked in a paralyzing struggle against one another. Those energies derive from three distinct modes of thought: the reductive, the creative, and the ecological.

The first, the reductive, might also be termed the analytic: its procedure is to take the object of study apart to see what it is made of and how it works. Its goal is to tease out the operations of a system into a single line of logic, so that

by following it anyone else would arrive inevitably at the
same conclusion, and the conclusions are clearly inherent in
the premises. This way of thought values the basic, the primary, the elementary, the simple; the single variable that
explains the workings of a complex system. And in fact this
analytic mode must always be exhausted or invalidated for
good reason before any other mode of thought can be ex-
pected to carry conviction; because analysis has the profound virtue of demonstrability, communicability, and
repeatability, and is thus accessible to every member of the
republic.

Such institutions as scientific experimental protocols,
international standards of weights and measures, the Food
and Drug Administration, scientific peer review periodicals,
repair and operation manuals, the Dewey decimal system of
library classification, due process of law, and so on are examples of the absolute necessity of the analytic mode, and its
indispensability in a democratic society. They also represent
a refreshingly noble objectivity in a world where desires are
equated with needs, and the truth is what we want it to be.
Science gets out the vote of the rest of the universe on what
it takes itself to be, not what we would have it be.

The analytic mode of thought has given us perhaps the
greatest practical gifts that we have received as a species. It
supplied the basis for our unprecedented control over the
rest of nature (though it could not provide a coherent conception of how or why we might exercise that control); it fed us,
it healed us, it clothed and housed us—it fulfilled all of Jesus'
great injunction when he bade us love our neighbor.

But the reductive mode has its deficiencies. It explains
wholes in terms of parts. It is deterministic: the outcome
must always be inherent in the origin, and thus it can look
only backwards into the past. It aspires to the absolute simplicity and automatism of the Big Bang. It values things only
for what they are made of and what they came from: the

parent is more valuable than the child, the origin than the result. Its law is one of decay, of a falling-off from an original richness of causal power to a decomposition of that power into more and more trivial and disordered threads of entropic consequence. Such things as mind are inaccessible to it; mind must be only a description of brain, and brain is only the mechanical workings of the neurons. It cannot accomodate that mysterious relationship between observer and observed which seems, in quantum theory, to close a loop in the universe between the most primitive and the most advanced constituents of it. It proceeds in the opposite direction from evolution, which is a process that works from past to future; its description of evolution has no language or concept for the emergence of new, richer forms of order and reflexiveness out of simpler, more primitive, more chaotic origins. Taken by itself, it would lead to a psychology in which we were neither free nor responsible, in which neither sin nor virtue had any meaning, and for which the creative inventions of both art and technology would be mere fantasies, random epiphenomena of a decaying world.

When natural reality starts working in even very simply nonlinear ways, as Prigogine and the Chaos theorists have shown, the analytic method must confront monstrosities like self-generating ordered systems, processes that forget their initial conditions, measurements whose increasing accuracy makes it more and more difficult, not easy, to predict the behavior of what is measured.

Analysis fails not only when it must confront evolving systems that develop emergent forms of order over time, but also when it looks at complex interdependent systems at any given moment of time. Its arrow of explanation points always backward, downward, down the slope of time, down the hierarchy of detail. But the horizontal arrow of relationship, of mutual influence, of those balance-restoring feedback systems that preserve an environment in a stable state, is invisible to the analytic eye. For the reductionist way of thought, the world is dead, and the chill perfections of death become the ideal yardstick against which life is measured. It can know neither the upward-pointing arrow of evolution, from parts to wholes, past to future, nor the horizontal arrow of mutual interdependence, of copresence, of system, of ecology, of culture.

And thus it is no surprise that the analytic mode, taken without sufficient alloy from other modes of thought, has got us into deep trouble. It is surely responsible in part for the quick-technical-fix, bottom-line attitude of much industrial exploitation of the environment, whether by free-enterprise business or socialist bureaucracy. It may yet be the destruction of the living world itself, whether by the ultimate reductiveness of the nuclear explosion, that reduces matter itself to energy, or by the slower process of beheading and poisoning the ecological body of Gaia. In economics, it has led to a reduction of all goods to crude numerical economic good, measured by money; a reduction which, alloyed in capitalist societies by the need to appeal to a consuming public, is totally unalloyed in leftist theory, where the welfare of various social groups (statistical phantoms such as Women, Minorities, the Poor, the Third World) is measured by a single monetary standard that degrades their culture, their personal value systems, and the actual complexities and differences of their way of life.

The reductive way of thought is by itself insufficient; though it is also absolutely necessary.

Let us turn, then, to a second mode of thought, that mode which proceeds in the same direction as evolution, from the simple to the complex, from past to future, from origins to new and unpredictable outcomes. This mode might be called the creative, the inventive, the progressive, the constructive, the synthesizing. In one sense, it is the optimistic and hopeful spirit of life itself, of sexual reproduction, of those enormous wasteful billowings of sperm and eggs—by the tons, the ten thousand tons—as the myriad-bodied organisms of the coral reefs release their great bet on the future two days after the full moon. Just so, a forest of chestnut trees will blossom hugely in the spring, the salmon will leap the falls to immolate themselves in their love death, the birds will build, the cats will yowl, the lovely young people blossom at the prom, the artist—Mozart even on his deathbed, Shakespeare three or four immortal plays in one year—will throw mind, body, and spirit into the fecund furnace of original creation. The creative impulse is at the heart of our purpose for being in the world: it is our freedom—freedom can be nothing else—and it is the only solution to the problem of desire.

The creative energy we see in the productions of biological evolution and human creativity can be found in an even more universal form, as the nonlinear positive feedback processes, dissipative systems, and self-organizing structures currently under investigation by Chaos science. Or perhaps we might broaden the term evolution to cover these processes, or say that evolution itself evolves, and that biology was just the first place where we noticed the phenomenon of evolution in general. Nature's own creativity, which we have come to know as generated by evolution, is not of a different kind from our own. Our thoughts are a new electrochemical way in which the old evolutionary process of creation can take place—but in us, the process is unimaginably faster and more powerful.

To this Promethean impulse can also be credited that effectuating and enabling vision by which science—passive and often reductive in itself—is transformed into technology. Let us celebrate for one last innocent moment the starry and heart-shaking glory of our technological civilization: the perfection, the sureness, the tautness of that entasis which springs the almost imperceptible arch of the pediment of the

Parthenon, the roadbed of the Golden Gate bridge; the fire of the rocket engines of the space shuttle *Challenger* as it rose into the blue Florida sky.

But the more technology has come to ignore and despise the past, to concentrate on the innovative, the futuristic, the efficiently productive, the more it has tended to exploit and despoil the natural and cultural environment, to destroy the past sources of value that help to maintain it. "History is bunk," said Henry Ford; a sentiment shared by the technological socialism of the eastern bloc countries, with their now-failed attempts to dissolve the heritage of religion, family, and culture. The forward-looking thought of the great artists and technologists is, alas, partly responsible for the ecological destruction that we cannot now ignore.

The trouble with the creative/innovative way of thought is that though indeed it does value things, it values them not for what they are but for what can be made of them, what they will result in. Modern galleries and museums of art all too often ignore work which is beautiful in itself in order to concentrate on the seminal breakthrough in concept or technique; the new is more valuable than the old, the old valuable only in that it anticipates the future. The older generation is oedipally sacrificed to the more advanced ideas of the new. In this form, the innovating way of thought is often deeply hostile to the scientific. Much polemic in the arts and the humanities has been directed against scientific reductionism and the linear thinking of the technocrats. And the reciprocal contempt of some established reductionists for the undisciplined thought of artists and visionaries is only too familiar.

The creative, innovative way of thought is indeed, *taken by itself,* deeply flawed. In desperation, then, we might be tempted to turn to the third great way of thought, the ecological, the relational, the present-oriented way of thought, as a panacea. Perhaps here we can find an answer, in that

gentle, loving realization that all is system, that we are all—
or if not, we should all be—equal participants in the world.
In this conception of things, the universe is a great network
or web of relations, and all entities in it are equally valuable.
Most important of all is the balance of nature, that self-
correcting equilibrium whereby any deviations are gently
corrected and all is adjusted to the common good.

And indeed, when we contemplate such natural phenomena as a coral reef, with its hundreds of thousands of
species living in relative harmony with each other—and its
beauty, its richness of forms, its mysterious order and its
innocent productiveness—we are almost persuaded that
that is how we human beings should live; or at least if we do
not live that way in some sense, we will not live at all. On
the social level, on the fringes of the academies, among certain groups of artists and intellectuals, a great experiment
in living this way is still going on, and its principles call forth
an aching loyalty even among those who do not live its practice. This way of life is one in which there is no hierarchy,
no distinction of persons, in which the good of each is identified with the good of all, in which an undiscriminating love
and acceptance bathes every member of the community, and
authority and prohibition are forever abolished.

In fields as diverse as ecological theory, general systems
theory, neomarxist economics, radical psychoanalysis, New
Age ethics, and the new moral theologies of the Christian
and Buddhist Left, the great ideal of the human community
in harmony with itself and nature is still pursued. We cannot deny the enormous transforming value of what it has
taught us.

But the social experiment of the sixties, which was designed to test these ideas, has, tragically, failed. For even
this way of thought, *taken by itself,* is dangerous and distorting. The commune ideal seemed to lead directly and unerr-
ingly toward the must brutal and bestial authoritarianism

or totalitarianism. Consider Jimmy Jones' idealistic community in Guyana, the happy equality and self-abnegation of
the Moonies, the name and mission of the Symbionese Liberation Army. Pol Pot was no doubt trying to create that non-
hierarchical kind of system in Cambodia, one in which the
population would all live in harmony with nature; and indeed the soil of Cambodia may well be richer with the organic fertilizer of those two million who died. Anyone who
has experienced the groupthink and ideological thought-po-
lice atmosphere of those college programs devoted to some
kind of minority-oriented revision of history will know the
phenomenon; and I have seen it at work in a consciousness-
raising group, a commune in Canada, and among environmental activists.

Why does this happen? Why should a way of thinking
devoted to the equality of all, to the unique value of the
individual, and to the common good, turn out again and
again to produce these monstrosities? The answer lies again
in the exclusion of the other necessary modes of thought—in
this case the reductive/analytical and the creative/innova-
tive. Ecological thought concerns itself with present horizontal relations between entities in systems, rather than the
downward vertical relation of a system to its past roots and
internal components, or its upward vertical relation with its
future, its goals, the greater whole of which it is a part. Thus,
ecological thought, taken by itself, tends to deny any differences of value between things, being capable only of relativistic evaluations depending on an arbitrarily-chosen point of
view within the great Web. This in practice means that the
ecological way of thought has no systematic way of assessing
greater or lesser value. The ecological mind cannot coherently prefer, for instance, the Weimar regime of Germany to
the Nazi regime that followed it. To do so would be to hie-
rarchize, which is anathema to the ecological mind. Strictly
speaking, such a person cannot coherently prefer his or her

*own* view to any other, but can only assert that they are different, and that one of them happens to be their own. Their values must thus be held without analysis, criticism, debate, or compromise, if they have any values at all. Hence the bigotry and prejudice of unexamined values must flourish when the ecological mode excludes the others.

Ecological thinking, moreover, is instinctively hostile to any kind of innovation; indeed, even to evolution, to the extent that evolution is an innovating process. The ecological way of thought is basically conservative; the only feedback processes it recognizes as legitimate are negative feedbacks which return a system to its original position. It fears both the linear processes of analysis and the nonlinear positive feedback processes of evolutionary creation, and it hates change. For innovation always unbalances an ecology, revises the terms of its relations, eliminates some participants and changes others. Evolution necessarily involves inequality—it is the very heart of inequality, since it works by differential rates of survival, competition, and clearly demonstrable inequities in reproductive success. Individuality itself, which is the driving force of evolutionary and artistic change, is the enemy. Those totalitarian communes flourish only because the members, their individuality diminished, reduced to a common equality of submission, are easy prey for some confident ideologue who can protect them from the fierce independence and individuality of people competing and cooperating outside in the real world.

Ecological thinking, taken by itself, is also deeply suspicious of science and of any knowledge of the parts, the past, and the development of the natural world as it is now. If a natural system has parts, then the parts must be unequal to the whole, and inequality enters in. If nature has a past, then it was not always thus, and there is nothing sacred about nature as it now stands (I can recall a radical ecologite reacting in blind fury to an inoffensive reference by a scientist to episodes of mass extinction in the past; it was as if holy scriptures were being violated). If nature has a development, the present system must be said to be better or at least more highly developed than its past, which implies that it might yet be improved upon.

For unalloyed ecological thought, the role of human beings in nature is to ignore the reflexive and dynamic capacities of the human mind, given to us by nature, and act as if we were merely one species of plants or animals among many in the garden, and not as the gardener or shepherd. In a paradoxical sense, the unalloyed ecological viewpoint is ecologically irresponsible. For if we are just another species in the system, why should we not do what all other species do when they get a chance: wipe out first all our competition and then all sources of our own nourishment? We can only protect the environment if we recognize that we are superior to it. Everything in the universe does indeed have vote in the constitution of the universe, as the ecologists insist; but it is not and should not be an equal vote.

For many reasons, then, we must reluctantly abandon pure and unalloyed ecological thought when it is taken by itself. Where, then, are we to turn?

It is by now clear that the answer is not simple, but is instead a plunge into a forbidding complexity—a recognition that we only see the world sanely and wholly when we see it with all three modes of thought at once: marveling at the scaled worlds within worlds of more and more elementary and deterministic elements that make it up, and from which it evolved; sharing in its own evolutionary/creative leap into freedom, transcendence, creation; and lovingly recognizing our participation and interdependence within the present ecology of the world.

Once we see the world in this larger, integrated way, it springs suddenly into three dimensions. The reductive mode of thought sees the world as a vertical timeline or scale of relative complexity, and privileges the bottom of the line—the most ancient, primitive, and elemental being the causal determinant of whatever happens higher up the line. The creative, synthesizing way of thought also uses the vertical timeline but privileges the top end of the line—the most recent and modern, the most advanced, the most constructed and intentional—and fears the past, historical or biological, as an infringement of our human freedom. The ecological way of thought sees the world as a flat plane covered with interrelated and equal entities, where nothing is privileged and therefore value judgments are impossible. But if we put all three together then we suddenly see the world as a dynamic evolutionary hierarchy, in which everything has value—the basic for being basic, the advanced for being the flowering and purpose of the basic; and there is plenty of room for those entities that share a given level of being to rejoice in their equality, intrinsic value, and interdependence.

What we see is an evolutionary ecology, a four-dimensional expanding manifold whose inside is the past, whose outside is the future, and whose expanding surface is the present. Every organism in the universe has its own vote in the constitution of the universe, as the ecologists assert. But that vote is weighted according to the complexity, integration, sensitivity and effective field of action of that organism, derived from its evolutionary history. Thus, in one breath, so to speak, is asserted forever both the greater value of those beings, human and other higher animals, that our moral intuition tells us to value highly above the insects, the plants, and the rocks; and the fundamental equality of all human beings, who share the same evolutionary history.

This vision of the world supplies us with an epistemology—a way of knowing—and an ethics of disagreement and coexistence. For, in this view, every opinion and argument is a member of an ecology of knowledge, where the competition and cooperation of its members produce a longterm increase in the richness and viability of the ecology as a whole. Bad opinions and arguments, like Nazism, will become extinct; good ones will survive to reproduce themselves. Such a view is consistent with democracy in politics, free enterprise in economics, and the dramatistic approach in aesthetics and sociology. It has its own systematic reasons for protecting the weak, the endangered species and the minority culture, as parts of the necessary symbiosis, and as rich repositories of genetic or cultural alternatives, which may be called on when the system as a whole must adapt to change.

What one loses when one takes on this combined mode of thought is the comfort of simplicity and partisanship, and a certain immediate political effectiveness, as one becomes more prone to see, with stark sympathy, the other person's point of view. What one gains is an enormous enfranchisement.

But the only way of learning to see the world in this fuller way is by actively engaging in a task which requires it. This is true both on the individual and the cultural level; but the value of an individual's work, as we have seen, is ultimately underwritten by the existence of a valid collective purpose: such as the terraforming of Mars. In this larger work the three modes of thought must be intimately combined, or success will be impossible. The transformation of Mars would be a necessary education to the human species: not only a scientific and technological exercise, but also an alchemical one. Its deepest meaning would be the spiritual metamorphosis of the alchemist.

And this is not a fantasy. The technology which is presently threatening the atmosphere and biosphere of Earth may one day be used to bring a dead planet to life. The biological metamorphosis of the planet Mars into one habitable by human beings now appears increasingly feasible. Several bodies of scientists are investigating various aspects of the problem, for instance, the Institute of Ecotechnics in London, Space Biospheres Ventures, the University of Arizona's Environmental Research Laboratory, the National Center for Atmospheric Research, the American Geophysical Union, Carl Sagan and his associates, and NASA. The ecological successes of such institutions as the Wisconsin Arboretum, which has recreated a virtually authentic prairie on degraded farmland, and Dan Jantzen's restored forest in Costa Rica, have encouraged efforts all over the world not just to protect but to create complex living ecosystems. Construction has begun on a sealed, self-sustaining, five million cubic foot environment in Arizona called Biosphere II.

James Lovelock, a distinguished British biologist, is the formulator of the Gaia Hypothesis, which maintains that the biosphere of Earth acts as a single organism to maintain the stability of the planet's atmosphere, oceanic environment, and temperature. His book (with Michael Allaby) entitled *The Greening of Mars,* outlines one strategy by which Mars might be transformed. Though one of his ideas—the use of chlorofluorocarbons or freons to produce a greenhouse effect on Mars—now seems impracticable, several elements of an even more ambitious, and perhaps quicker, solution to the problem already exist.

First is the revolution which has recently occurred in our understanding of Earth's early evolution. The original atmosphere of Earth would be highly lethal to contemporary living organisms, being composed largely of hydrogen sulfide, methane, and ammonia, with almost no free oxygen. The first living organisms were anaerobes, that is, life-forms which do not need free oxygen and would indeed by poisoned by exposure to it. However, free oxygen was excreted by many early organisms as a waste product, rather as we and our technology excrete carbon dioxide. When the available "oxygen sinks"—metallic ores, for instance, that could soak up oxygen in the formation of oxides, or hydrogen, which combined with oxygen to create much of the water of the earth's oceans—were exhausted, the new oxygen atmosphere poisoned the old anaerobic organisms that had brought it into being, leaving only those forms of life, such as the blue-green algae or cyanobacteria, which could either endure the presence of oxygen or, better still, use it as an enhanced energy source for photosynthesis, the creation of sugars, and the metabolic extravagances of the more advanced animals. With this change came the age of the eukaryotes, those organisms whose nucleated structure was such as to promote multicellular organization and sexual reproduction.

If this transformation could occur on Earth by biological means, might it not also be made to happen on Mars? Of course, the process took hundreds of million years on Earth; but Earth had to make do with the very primitive and haphazard organisms supplied by its early evolution, whereas today there exists an enormous riches of life-chemistries and metabolisms to draw on.

But no contemporary Earth organism could survive long on Mars, whose carbon dioxide atmosphere is at a pressure less than one hundredth of the Earth's—not enough to allow liquid water to exist—whose surface temperature, averaging -40 degrees Fahrenheit, can support frozen carbon dioxide, and which because of its thin atmosphere and weak magnetic field is bombarded by ultraviolet radiation. Nonetheless, certain Earthly organisms—bacteria, for the most part—can handle conditions nearly as severe as these when taken one by one, though none can withstand them taken all together. Enormous advances are now taking place in bioengineering, whereby traits deemed desirable can be grafted from one organism to another. Could not hardened strains, chimeras, be generated, that might be adapted to the Martian environment? But in order to metabolize and reproduce, such organisms would need water.

The terrain of Mars clearly shows that at certain points of its geological history water has flowed on its surface. It could again, if the temperature of the planet could be raised sufficiently to release gases locked up as ice and increase the pressure to the point that free water could exist. Various methods for doing this have been proposed. By means of dyes, artificial dust clouds or pigmented living organisms, the albedo—reflectivity—of the Martian surface could be reduced, so that less radiation was leaving its atmosphere than was striking it. So to turn Mars green, it would first be necessary to make it black.

Robert Parke, an Australian Mars expert and visionary, suggests that the Martian moon Phobos might be used as a source of raw materials. The best hypothesis as to its composition is that its top few hundred feet is composed of very dark material, that could be fired by sun-powered electric mass-drivers against Phobos's weak gravitation (one thousandth that of Earth) into the gravitational field of Mars, where it would either spread throughout the atmosphere or be aimed to fall on the polar regions. Here, the dark material would absorb nearly twenty times as much heat as the water and carbon dioxide ices of the polar caps, and the sun's heat would begin to vaporize the caps, much as it does Halley's comet in photographs by Russian, Japanese, and European spacecraft. Other larger chunks of Phobos material, from deep under its surface, rich in frozen water, ammonia, and organic materials, could be impacted on the Martian surface, especially near Mars' ancient river and lake beds, which contain more locked-up water and organic sediments. These chunks would constitute artificial meteors, and their impact would vaporize the water and organics, create greenhouse-effect dust clouds, and heat the planet's mantle. Perhaps the old volcanoes of Mars would become active once more, adding their outgassing to the atmosphere.

Many of the necessary changes on Mars might employ

the new concept of nanotechnology, whereby tiny self-reproducing chemical factories can be programmed for specific tasks, such as the mining and extraction from the Martian soil of the necessary gases. But in a sense this is only another extension of the idea of the Von Neumann machine, the machine which can make copies of itself; we already possess a fantastic riches of such machines, and we call them Life.

Or, one might use even more radical solutions. The Saturnian ice-moon S26, recently and suggestively renamed Pandora, is about a hundred kilometers in diameter, giving a volume of about half a million cubic kilometers, and a mass of about 500 thousand trillion tons. If half this mass were used as the reaction mass to drive the other half, it might be shifted from its orbit enough to enter the gravitational fields of other satellites of Saturn, be slingshot out of Saturn's gravity well and made to fall upon the planet Mars. Even if only a fraction of the gases released by the impact were to remain in the Martian atmosphere, such a collision could raise the pressure and temperature of the Martian surface considerably: enough to make it geologically and climatologically live. It would also be the most spectacular event ever created by human beings. Each meter of Earth's surface supports about twenty tons of air and an average of about two thousand tons of water. Pandora would provide a comparable amount of gases and liquids for each square meter of Mars. If this gigantic feat of engineering is beyond our powers, Saturn has many smaller moons, and once freed from their primary orbits they could coast without further attention to their fiery rendezvous on Mars.

Even now the project seems hopeless to a twentieth-century technological imagination. Nature has had billions of years to try out different life-forms for their survival possibilities; jerrybuilt germs are notoriously fragile outside the laboratory and incapable of survival in the field. But suppose evolution itself could be speeded up, in controlled conditions that would gradually approximate those of Mars, so that the Martian strains could, so to speak, generate themselves? The limits of metabolism forbid this; but they do not forbid software simulacra from doing so.

Contemporary computer biologists are already developing ways to express the genetic and somatic structure of simple organisms as computer programs. The next stage would be to place those programs together in a large cybernetic environment where they can compete and evolve for selective fitness; and thus speed up the process of evolution electronically by many orders of magnitude. Gradually, the simulated conditions could be altered from those of an Earthly environment to those of Mars. In the struggle for survival, certain traits would be selected for, generation by swift generation, and the genes which code for them could be carefully recorded. It now begins to appear that the 95% of the DNA in the genes of living organisms which is not expressed constitutes a rich archive of their evolutionary history, and may contain exquisite mechanisms that could be tried out swiftly in such an environment and perhaps used in the work of synthesis. What is learned in this way could then guide recombinant DNA engineering to produce very hardy strains. The obvious dangers of this work would be mitigated by forms of testing which threaten not a real, but a modeled and cybernetic/imaginary environment.

Many of the components of such a project are already in existence. Followers of the computer games section of the *Scientific American* will be familiar with some of them: Conway's Game of Life, the Core Wars battle programs that fight it out for possession of a memory space, certain expert systems that can learn from experience and adapt themselves accordingly, genetic algorithms, biomorphs, and the new iterative or chaotic algorithms that can generate complex internal electronic environments. Meanwhile, computer modeling is now being used extensively in molecular biology, cytology, and ecology; and the National Science Foundation is currently proposing the creation of a complete record of the human genome, that is, our full complement of DNA base-pairs in their correct order, divided into chromosomes: all the information needed to construct a human being (and perhaps its evolutionary past). Several viruses and bacteria have already been thus recorded by gas chromatography in whole or in part. The techniques of genetic/cybernetic manipulation could also be used to tailor plants to grow into shapes useful to human beings, like the Martian dwellings in our example.

By some combination of these methods, then, organisms adapted to life on Mars might be synthesized. But would it not take an enormous amount of time to propagate them over the Martian surface? Here, the astonishing mathematics of reproduction would be heavily in favor of the planetary gardeners. Normal bacteria can reproduce themselves by fission in as little as twenty minutes; conservatively, let us estimate ten doublings per day for tailored bacteria. In one day a ton of bacteria, finely scattered over a surface rich in nutrients, and without biological competition, could yield a thousand tons—about a thousand cubic meters—of biomass; in five days, this mass, if unimpeded by lack of raw materials, would approach one hundred trillion tons. The surface of Mars is about 146 million square kilometers in extent— roughly a hundred trillion square meters. Thus, in this ideal case, it would take five days to cover the whole surface of Mars with bacteria to a depth of a meter, starting with one ton of seed. One might rest both on the sixth and seventh days. Of course, the vicissitudes of access to food chemicals and energy sources, as well as unfavorable local variations in temperature, pressure, etcetera—some of them brought about by the bacterial growth itself—would put a stop to this growth very swiftly. But the illustration shows the potency of the biological instrument the colonists could wield.

One generation of bacterial species would certainly not be enough; the first generation would have to be used as the compost for the second, the second for a third, and so on. At some point cyanobacteria, which excrete oxygen, would be introduced. Other bacteria produce nitrogen. Each generation would at first be smothered by its own waste-products, but the net effect would be to extract from the Martian atmosphere and regolith (rock soil) the carbon dioxide necessary to sustain a greenhouse effect and the water, oxygen, and nitrogen that constitute an Earth-type environment. Oxygen in the stratosphere would be broken up by sunlight to form a protective ozone layer against the ultraviolet. Shallow seas would form, and corals could be sown in them to begin the process by which the level of atmospheric carbon dioxide is controlled.

After a while, hardy funguses and plants could be introduced, then the grasses and the higher flowering plants, the angiosperms, together with the insects to pollinate them. Next would come the higher animals, and finally human beings, the new homesteaders—families with their seed catalogs, their hand tools, and the prospects of a new nation and a new dispensation for humankind. And no native tribe would have been displaced or murdered; no living species would have paid by extinction for human progress.

What might Mars, so transformed, be like to live in?

Southeastwards, in the direction you came from this morning, you can see sloping tablelands of forest broken and stepped with precipices banded with blood red, ocher, and brown, in shadow still from the tiny sun. They fall off northwards to an ocean that looks somehow wrong—the waves are too short and too tall, like the stylized waves in an old theater, worked to and fro to give the illusion of movement (with a fat-lipped dolphin, perhaps, and a little galleon). The waves are blue on the lit side, but deep pink on the shadow side. The

ocean is scattered with islands as yet unnamed, rings or
semicircles of green; but beyond them looms up into the
violet sky a vague outline of impossible scale: the last ring-
wall of the Pandora Crater System where the largest of the
human-made meteors struck forty years ago.

As you turn west, the albedo changes, the sky now purple opposite the sun, and here the mesas of the Nilosyrtis
rise like pink ghosts, their faces lit by the dim sunlight. The
cliffs are iced like a cake with groves of gigantic trees, silver
trunks, emerald leaves—English beeches, it looks like, but of
giant size. Waterfalls drift down into the ravine below, with
a dreamlike slowness, breaking into vapor with a soft hiss as
they hit the rocks. Above the hills, clouds are beginning to
form—tall, billowy, ramshackle columns like stovepipes or
chef's hats. The turf under your feet is covered with fresh
little flowers, and mixed with their earthy scent there is a
smell strange and intimate, like raw milk, iron, sulfur, and
snow-water.

Southwards, the mountains rise and rise again, and as
you turn, the Gulf of Isis comes into view again, hung over
by the tiny blazing sun. The light is like a rich and brilliant
twilight, or the dimmed glow of a warm winter noon in
northern Europe; or perhaps like the light of an acadian
painting, Poussin or Claude. The painter cannot lay a
brighter pigment than her whitest white on the canvas, and
she knows that even that white must be diminished by the
glazes and varnish; so she darkens every color in her palette
to a velvet chiaroscuro, softens all the details in the shade,
and saves the sharpness and the clarity for the ship caught
in the blaze of noon beside the rocky cave in the bay; and
makes the arbutus leaves glow as if backlit, and keeps her
best clot of white for the bright lozenge of sea and sky where
the painting's lines meet at the vanishing point.

The vanishing point here on Mars, though, is strangely
close. It's an oddly cozy world, despite the wildness with

which nature here strews her fresh designs about—nature here informed by human art and intention. The horizon is very close, and the rich vapor and dust, much of it organic and alive, with which the colonists have seeded the new atmosphere to keep the greenhouse effect at work, makes for intimate landscapes. It's like the misty air of England, but with Mars' characteristic pinkish tinge, from the dominance of the iron oxides.

You could have got to this place flying under your own power, for you weigh three eighths of what you weigh on Earth, and with appropriately designed wings and some training you could realize the ancient human dream of being free of the ground. Here, on Mars, you can leap to twice your height, and long-jump over thirteen meters, with a hang-time of nearly three seconds. Wearing the wings, you find you have time to take two strokes, which gives you a glide you can maintain. Then you can get your feet into the stirrups and use the powerful leg muscles to get your flying height. A hundred meters keeps you out of trouble, and you still have good depth perception. Landing can be a problem, and takes practice. They can start you on the brained wings which do it for you—"drop the flaps," as they say—extend and cup the primary feathers, open the secondaries, and stall out just as you hit the ground.

Or you can go higher, by finding a thermal or an updraft where the prevailing wind blows up over a ridge; and get out of earshot of the ground, to where you can no longer hear people talking, animals stamping and snorting, the rush and burble of the streams, the sigh of trees, the sound of bells and music. It gets very silent, though you can still smell the grass smell of the hot meadow below. And there you are, up in the sunny blisses of the middle air, feeling your eardrum pop with the altitude, with a fantastic choice of detail from the whole hemisphere of world beneath, the foreshortened hillocks, the strange organic shapes of Martian homesteads (grown by recombinant DNA out of living trees), brackish streams flashing suddenly with sunlight as they meander sluggishly through multicolored bogs toward the new sea. And down the coast, maybe the art deco villas and palms and awnings of a little seaside resort. Perhaps it is its own little Jeffersonian republic, or perhaps it has a form of government for which we do not have a name. You could go there now, but you don't want to leave the air, which has become for you a school of joy. The problem is not how to get up any more, it's how to get down.

Consider the ancient Greeks in their eye-painted ships, feeling their way along the monstrous volcanic coast of Italy, until they came to the apocalyptic landscape of Vesuvius: the huge canted ash-cone of the crater, the island fragments—Ischia, Capri—of a great caldera whose head blew off before history began, the Hadean barrens of the Solfatara, the hellmouth lake of Avernus whose fumes would kill any bird that flew over it. This place was a Mars for the colonizing Greeks. They founded cities on the coast—Paestum, Cumae—and dug caves there to house their oracles, their holy women. They found ways to garden a crater planetscape. There the Cumaean Sibyl spoke to Aeneas and prophesied the Roman Empire, and there also, if Virgil speaks the truth, she foretold the coming of Jesus of Nazareth. Dante knew that infernal landscape too: only by that way could he reach the divine spaceworlds of Paradise.

We too, like Greek or Trojan wanderers, have a mission to carry our sacred scriptures and household gods—our DNA, our ecosphere, our poetry—into a new world where they may be preserved and transformed. If Gaea is the mother-goddess who nursed us, we are offered the chance to give birth to the daughter-goddess of another planet.

# THE ART OF
# ARTIFICIAL
# INTELLIGENCE

RECENT PROCLAMATIONS OF THE death of history are exaggerated; the old agendas, of collective spiritual salvation, the liberation and equality of humankind, international law and order, ecological hygiene, and social justice, are unfinished business enough to occupy us for a few millenia yet. But where such goals are immediately achievable, they do not require much mental ingenuity or imagination. And, for the most part, they are not immediately achievable, but require huge and pervasive changes in our vision of the world, our collective aspirations, our moral, artistic, and scientific horizons. We need new challenges to make us embark on those changes, to catch our imaginations, to evoke our ingenuity.

What new challenges can we propose to recharge the

engines of history? One, which I have already suggested, is the extension of the living ecology of our planet to the dead worlds of the solar system, involving an increase of knowledge and awareness of living systems that would be necessary if we are to save Earth itself.

Another project which might galvanize our collective imaginative energies is the search for artificial intelligence. Here one must at once concede that as presently conceived, there is little in this project to attract the talents and enthusiasm of anyone outside a small circle of software experts, computer nerds, and robot enthusiasts. Moreover, the quest seems recently to have lost its impetus, becalmed by a lack of new ideas, stranded in the complex shoals of technology, and swept backwards by the intimidating magnitude of a task at first thought of as simple.

But AI (the normal acronym) is still, whether we like it or not, the next great intellectual frontier. The constituents of the universe are, going from the simplest to the most complex: number, field, energy, matter, life, and mind. We can be said to have at least an inkling as to how field is made of number, energy of field, matter of energy, life of matter; and each of these relationships required a heroic intellectual breakthrough to reveal, and each had enormous effects upon society. The last challenge is to see how mind emerges out of this whole sequence, and to duplicate that emergence so that we know we have got it right.

Let us try to look at the whole issue of artificial intelligence anew. A naive and non-technical redefinition of the problem may reconnect it with the grand themes and interests of the culture at large, and may even suggest untried avenues of research.

How would we know if we'd got artificial intelligence, when we'd got it? The classical response to this question is the Turing Test, which is a conversation by typed messages with the putative intelligent machine. If you cannot tell whether you are communicating with a person or a machine, the machine is intelligent. In other words, we know we have artificial intelligence when the machine understands and can use natural language.

The sciences of computer hardware and software go back scarcely a century, to Charles Babbage or perhaps to Joseph Jacquard in 1801, whose coded instructions to his new loom, to weave the lovely paisleys that bear his name, are considered the first true software program. But there is a field which, for the last five thousand years at least, has been at work on precisely the issue that is crucial and central to artificial intelligence: what it means to understand and to be able to speak a natural language. That field is literature.

If we asked a literary expert who was also computer-literate what it takes to understand natural language, the answer might take the form of the following recipe. (Some ingredients may be hard to find.)

First, you need a massive database: that is, enormous amounts of sheer knowledge. Now knowledge is not a passive thing, random access memory stored in the same form in which it was put in. What we call knowledge is actually two things: skills, or habits of action; and memory, that is, a capacity to recreate or regenerate an earlier experience, using an awareness of the generative principles of what is remembered together with some significant fragment of the original whole that can serve as a seed and test of the result. We seem to reconstitute our memories by a method not unlike the way in which an iterated computer program can generate a complex fractal shape out of a simple mathematical seed or algorithm. But we also seem to need a background awareness of the whole world as the context and editor of the reconstructed memory; the remembered experience must fit into the right-shaped hole in everything else, and this fit acts as another check of its accuracy. The way a memory fits in is essentially as part of a story, a program of contemplated or imagined action, which gives point and application to the knowledge. Thus, knowledge, either as a skill of action or as memory, is essentially active and creative.

Together with this massive database, you must have a massively complex information processing capacity that is not clearly distinguished from the database itself: what we call the power of thought. J. T. Fraser has calculated the number of possible brain states in a human brain—its repertoire—to be of the order of ten raised to the power of ten raised to the power of nine: that is, one followed by a billion zeroes. To write this number down, you would need a hundred books. It is much larger than the number of particles in the universe. The processing method itself is not of a single kind, but is a huge collection of different kinds of organization—logical, probabilistic, holographic, symbolic, metaphorical, metonymic, and so on.

Next, this whole collection must be unified into a single self, which sits at the top of a "chunked" hierarchy of labeled subunits referencing, controlling, and sensitive to smaller and smaller moieties of the whole. One of the most amazing characteristics of intelligence is its simplicity and unity, achieved only if all its functions can be concentrated and subsumed into a single focus of attention.

Further, the process must be enormously flexible. Its input must be able to alter its programming (learning); the program must be able to alter the hardware (habit); the program and the hardware must be able to be fed back into the system as input (introspection and psychological inquiry); and the higher-level functions must be subjected to periods of partial immersion in their own lower-level processing (dream).

And the whole system must be fully integrated into a world suited to its capacities, by means of its distribution into a sensing, feeling, and active controllable body. A large part of intelligence consists in the informative interplay between an information processor and its world. That world must itself be highly complex, partly intelligible, and composed of a mixture of predictable and unpredictable elements. Without such a world, the intelligent system could not learn and would be paralyzed with boredom.

These ingredients must in turn be cooked together in such a way as to generate emergent properties of a reflexive and self-organizing kind. These include a circular feedback/feedforward loop (consciousness, self-awareness); self-inclusion paradoxes (mystical experience and the higher tenses of time); iterative, chaotic, non-linear relationships with the world (drama, personal history, humor).

The result should be capable of originality: consciousness is a reality generator. And originality constitutes freedom, because in changing the world it changes the choices the world offers. Consciousness is unpredictable (though after the fact its decisions can make perfect sense), autonomous (self-ordering), and creative.

Interestingly enough, these characteristics that define intelligence—massive database, massive complexity of information processing, unity, flexibility, feedback and self reference, originality, freedom—also add up to a rather convincing definition of the quality traditionally called Beauty. Why? We will need to return to this question after further thought.

But, at first glance, it would certainly appear that if all these criteria and conditions must be met by a machine, then artificial intelligence is impossible. Indeed, they could be read as a way to debunk the idea of artificial intelligence.

Far from it. If artificial intelligence is impossible, then natural intelligence must be impossible too, for exactly the same reasons. How could all that power be packed into a one-quart skull? How could this mess of chemical and electrical connections produce creative imagination, a self, a soul? And how could the extremely variable, inexact, and almost haphazard process of cellular development produce intelligence almost every time a human zygote is allowed to mature?

But natural intelligence does not come full-blown into the world. It relies on an animal body and sensorium already provided by billions of years of evolution and heredity; it requires a world to develop in, a family, a culture, an education. Indeed, if the latter are present, a specifically human body and nervous system are not absolutely necessary; Koko the gorilla knows some human language, which we have established as the benchmark for intelligence. And if a world, family, culture, and education are absent, as they are for human babies that are fed and housed but otherwise neglected, a human being, suffering from what is sometimes called kwashiorkor or marasmus, may never learn as much language, or be as "human," as Koko. The machine of the living brain is not sufficient for intelligence; why should an electronic machine be sufficient either? If "natural" intelligence is permitted a highly complex machine to run on—that is, a sensorium, a body, a family, a culture, a world—then why should we not grant the same conditions to "artificial" intelligence?

Another, more radical way of making this point is to say that the distinction between natural and artificial intelligence is itself artificial, and may in many senses be plain wrong. All living organisms, including even viruses (which exploit the biochemical machinery of other lifeforms), use tools to survive and could not make it using only their own bodies. The water in which a bacterium swims is a kind of tool. But even bodies are a kind of tool. As far as the genes are concerned, the whole complicated structure of protein chemicals that constitutes the body of an animal or plant is a machine designed to ensure the survival of the genes. The nervous system is a piece of complex wiring created over eons of evolutionary time to protect and serve the body as a whole; and its emergent properties of consciousness, individuality, and so on are a kind of technology. Natural intelligence *is* artificial, in this sense; the problem of artificial intelligence has already been solved, and all we need to do is understand and duplicate the solution.

One implication of this way of looking at the issue is that there may be forms of intelligence that inhabit our complex technological, biological, and institutional machinery other than the persons who are christened, vote, get married, and play the central role in funerals. Even within a single human body there can often be several centers of conscious awareness. Consider the various consciousnesses of a split personality patient. They are clearly distinct intelligences, and often have different tested I.Q.. (Should each one have the right to vote? If not, do we deny the franchise to the Republican or to the Democratic personality?) Or consider the introjected and internalized personality of a parent or other family member, or one of the beloved dead. At their best, such persons are for many of us a dear presence with whom we can talk. At their worst, they can be like the elder Mrs. Bates in *Psycho*. In any case, they have a great deal of spontaneous and individual intelligence, quite distinct from the mind of the person that harbors them. Or what about the self that is criticized when we criticize ourselves? It is not the self that criticizes. You fool, we say to ourselves. You fool, for calling yourself a fool.

When one converses with another person one must construct an internal model of that person's consciousness, with its own independent motivations, in order to be able to converse with him or her at all. That internal model must have its own internal model of oneself, with its own internal model of the other person, and so on. And if one is a writer of fiction, one will often find, if one is any good, that the characters one has created have, as we say, taken on a life of their own, and can engage in a battle of wills with their creator. A good actor can become consumed by the role he plays. The role, the fictional character, can surprise its author as thoroughly as any person of flesh and blood.

And here we enter the world of all those intelligences that are carried and mediated collectively and institutionally, whether they were once living persons, or were created by artists, shamans, politicians, cartoonists, or advertisers: Uncle Sam, Falstaff, Florence Nightingale, Wild Bill Hickock, Liberty, Santa Claus, Jesus, Athena, Buddha, the Jolly Green Giant, the battleship Big Mo; the gods, goddesses and heroes; the patron saints; the presences that haunt rivers and groves, gallows and childbirths; the spirits of nations; and the commercial corporate personalities to which Locke and Hobbes granted semi-legal reality, and which we tax, criticize, sue, and reward.

These various entities form a continuous series in which it is rather hard to draw a strict line of demarcation separating genuine independent intelligences from "mere" fictions. If they are intelligent, they are not the same intelligences as the human beings that support them. I would maintain that they are perfectly adequate examples of existing artificial intelligence. They live, like parasites or symbiotes or viruses, upon the host circuitry of individual people or groups of people, using much of their working hardware and even input, but transforming it in ways unavailable to the unaided host. But in this they do not differ from the human beings themselves, which live as symbiotes upon their own bodies, their culture, their language, their world. Are these artificial persons self-aware? Do they possess subjectivity? Some of them clearly do, like the split personalities of the mental patient; and many actresses will tell you that they have experienced, say, Cleopatra's own motivations and self-hood from the inside. With the Easter Bunny, Britannia, and the Pillsbury Doughboy, the question is more problematic but not utterly ridiculous.

These secondary intelligences even have a dormant existence in books, musical scores, paintings stored in attics, and so on. They are activated when they are played on a human brain, using the brain tissue as their hardware.

In the last few years a number of computer researchers involved in artificial intelligence and information architecture have become students of the humanities. It seemed to them that the cybernetic disciplines themselves did not have a rich enough body of theory and sufficient practical experience with the nature of Mind to be able to solve the new and interesting problems that lay beyond expert systems, symbolic logic, and holographic image-recognition. Artificial neural networks, the new hardware approach to artificial intelligence in which electronic systems were designed to mimic the human brain, had bogged down in an atmosphere of caution and pessimism, and a disinclination to set the sights higher than the solution of immediate practical problems. Some AI researchers came to the arts and the humanities looking for a wider conceptual structure. In the process, they have suggested new creative directions for those traditional disciplines.

One of these researchers, whom I know well, visited the Impressionists in the Kimbell Museum of Art, and he came back with a visionary gleam in his eye. "It's AI!" he said. He had seen a Cézanne and found himself hooked into another worldview, another way of thinking, a new subjectivity. It was not just AI, but telepathy. The light on that jumble of rooves across the Seine, the strange, lovely, drear feeling of that afternoon, and then the oddly pastoral thoughts, the sense of the city as a sort of countryside, transcended all those years, the language barrier, the valley of the shadow of death. People who translate foreign poetry into their own language can similarly feel from the inside the subjectivity of the poet they serve, the spontaneity of his wit and feeling, and are sometimes not sure whether what they are feeling comes from themselves or from their poet. And is not a violin solist transformed into the Mozart she plays, perhaps into something that is more Mozart than Mozart was himself most of the time?

We already have artificial intelligence. The arts are traditional forms of artificial intelligence going back some tens of thousands of years. This is not a metaphor, and it arguably constitutes the most accurate definition of art itself. Milton said that a book is the precious lifeblood of a master spirit. This is not mere rhetoric. Poems, paintings, novels, sculpture, music are artificial intelligence programs to be run on human computers.

Not that the cybernetic search for AI is a waste of time, a reinvention of the wheel. An analogy with biological science may be helpful. When the DNA code was discovered, and then recombinant DNA techniques opened the way to direct manipulation of the genes, it looked as if we were stepping into utterly new territory. Some of us were exhilarate, many were terrified. What monsters might we produce? But then we gradually realized that human beings have been doing slow DNA manipulation by selective breeding and hybridization for thousands of years already, and that wheat, dogs, sheep, apples, and cattle were all artificial species. Further, the research of people like Lynn Margulis showed that all bacteria were already quite happily, and in the most polymorphously perverse way, exchanging genetic material in a continuous incestuous group grope; and that through viral insertions into our own genes we too were part of the same millenial orgy. *We* were the chimeras, the Frankenstein's monsters, the Andromeda Strain. And so were all our brothers and sisters in the animal and vegetable kingdoms.

But this did not imply that, because nature was doing it already, we should give up recombinant DNA research. All it meant was that our research was an absolutely natural continuation of nature's own research and experimentation, and further, that we now had the most expert and ancient guides in our work. Those who hate and fear science and technology often like to offer the choice between power, knowledge, and control on one hand, and harmonious, natural, organic relationships on the other. It turns out that we can have both, and in fact the more power and knowledge we have, the further we go along Nature's own path. Laboratory DNA splicing is only a faster and more controllable version of the gene shuffling which happens outside the lab, but there are advantages to speed and control. A new feedback process—that is, conscious knowledge and decision—will have been added to the already rich brew of evolutionary self-organization.

The same applies to artificial intelligence research. The universe itself is an artificial intelligence research project, and this planet is one of its laboratories. The animals were the first successes in the project, and they became the laboratory subjects for the next phase. When some of those laboratory animals discovered Art, they discovered how to induce artificial intelligence in themselves. Now they are trying to induce it in forms of matter other than the carbon-hydrogen-nitrogen-oxygen machines in which it first arose; perhaps it can be done in silicon doped with metallic impurities. Perhaps not. But the process is entirely in the spirit of nature and a continuation of it; in a sense, a natural duty. Some theologians maintain that this physical world is the body of God; if this is so, it needs a nervous system. Perhaps we are the agents, in God's own fetal development, by which the world's body is to be innervated and rendered sensitive, passionate, and self-aware.

Is AI in the old sense, possible? I believe it is, if the question means, "Is it possible to build hardware that will match the power, connectivity, and architectural sophistication of the human brain?" Current developments in the speed, complexity, flexibility, and architecture of cybernetic devices show continuous exponential improvements. Massively parallel architectures, connection machines, laser systems for connecting components, artificial neural networks, direct neural-cybernetic interfaces, tunneling transistors, superconducting circuitry, hardware laid down in and by genetically-engineered living systems, and so on, are all in the pipeline. At some point, the sheer numerical complexity of a cybernetic system will surpass that of a human brain.

But will this be enough? Can a computer match the capacities of a human mind? The answer here must be, "No." A computer is what is called a "Turing machine," that is, a device which carries out the commands of a program or algorithm. Its workings are in principle predictable, linear, and deterministic, and it cannot generate any kind of order which is not implicit in its input. The only kind of truth it "knows" is the kind that it can prove. Human beings, however, without resorting to any mystical assertions of supernatural powers, regularly deal with truths they cannot prove. For instance, as the great mathematician Kurt Gödel showed, the statement "This statement is not provable" is true, and we can know that it is true; but it is not provable, for if so it would not be true! The reason why we can know that "This statement is not provable" is that we can step outside any system of proof, any group of axioms, and recognize global properties of the system or group as a whole. In other words, our minds are infinitely expandable; they can generate new perspectives not predictable from the old. The artistic power of creative imagination is thus the first requisite for any knowledge of truth!

Does this mean that AI is impossible? How might we build creative imagination, unpredictability, infinite expandability—in other words, freedom—into a machine? If the natural sciences stood now where they did up to a few decades ago, the project would be impossible by definition. The universe was made up of deterministic processes interfering with each other in ways which could be calculated and predicted. Perhaps there was an irreducible element of "noise"—of random vibration—in any system, but even this property was at last reduced into the statistical descriptions of quantum theory. Chance and necessity—that was all there was. Philosophers, artists, and spokespersons of the human spirit were reduced to one of two desperate measures to assert the dignity and freedom of humanity. One was to posit a supernatural world in which freedom could exist but which, unfortunately, required the abandonment of reason. The other was to equate freedom with sheer chance, sheer randomness; and hence we got the existentialist's "acte gratuite," the gratuitous act of Camus' and Sartre's heroes. Even now, artists, in an attempt to escape what they imagine to be the deterministic and mechanistic tyranny of reality, resort to aleatory or chance-based processes in their creations.

But the great revolution in scientific thinking through which we have just passed has changed all this. Biological systems are not the only ones which involve feedback, nonlinearity, and self-transforming flexibility. There is a whole new class of mathematics which describes and generates nonlinear, nondeterministic, discontinuous processes. Whole new branches of physics and chemistry have arisen that deal with open systems, self-organizing processes, infinitely self-transforming feedback loops, ordered entities whose initial conditions can no longer be extracted even in theory, and whose future behavior, without being in any sense random, is beyond the capacity of any calculator, even one made of the whole universe, to predict. The universe is itself free, autonomous, creative, self-transcending, self-ordering. Our conscious awareness and will are not an anomaly in the world but simply the intensest form of nature's own self-reflective and self-generating process; and the evolution that brought us about is only a slower version of the same creative investigation that revealed the nature of evolution itself.

The physical world, then, already provides many processes that in principle give us the ingredients of a creative, free, and expandable artificial intelligence. There are already software programs that, within certain narrow limits, can mimic the unpredictable genesis of order that we find in living systems. Beginning with Conway's game of Life and the fractal sets of Benoit Mandelbrot and his followers, a whole new class of iterative computer programs has been devised, which reproduce the chaotic self-organization of nonlinear physical systems and the fantastic creativity of biological evolution. New cybernetic entities called bi-omorphs are, even now, happily reproducing themselves in competition with their fellow-survivors, within the memory-spaces of private, business, and educational computers. They "live" within Turing machines, but are not Turing machines themselves.

For living organisms to evolve, three basic factors must be present: some mechanism of variation that ensures that each new generation will display significant departures in form and function from its ancestors; a process of selection whereby an environment (which may include the presence and interactions of the species itself) can eliminate from the breeding population those organisms not fit to survive in it; and a conserving mechanism of heredity, to fix in a genetic archive what has been learned in the process itself. This archive must in turn be subject to variation in the next generation, providing a field within which selection can go to work, the results recorded by the differential preservation of some genes over others, and so on.

The iterative, feedback nature of this process is crucial. One cycle of the process is not enough. But the sequence of many cycles generates a self-organizing flow which tends toward what chaos theoreticians call a "strange attractor," a complex but ordered shape of remarkable integrity, dura-bility, and beauty. Throughout nature—in the shapes of tur-bulent flow, the orbits of complex star-systems, the organization of the human heartbeat, the precipitation of crystals out of a melt, the dissipation of electric charges, the branchings of trees and ferns, the storm-systems and anticyclones of world weather, the great red spot of Jupiter—strange attractors seem to call ordered shapes out of random but connected chaos. We find those shapes especially pleasing, whether they occur in the spirals of shells, the tails of sea-horses, the seedpods of plants, or in the imitated organic forms of Jacquard paisleys. Earlier on in this essay, we discovered that the definition of intelligence corresponded rather strangely with a good definition of beauty. Perhaps this is because our pan-human capacity for beauty is a natural recognition of free self-organizing reflexive feedback systems and an ability to create them.

Like the outcome of a good story, an attractor is not predictable from the initial conditions or from the algorithm (for instance, the variation-selection-heredity cycle), but once it has begun to appear out of the apparently random results of the process, it makes perfect sense. We can tell whether a process is genuinely alive and organic by the suspense we feel as it works itself out, a suspense that comes from knowing that whatever shape appears cannot be predicted but will be ingeniously adapted to its conditions. No suspense, no life.

It might well be said that each living species is itself a kind of strange attractor, the natural but unpredictable goal of a given set of genetic inheritances combined with a given ecological niche. Hence, for instance, anteaters of similar shape and capabilities have evolved independently on three continents, and hence also the remarkable convergence in form and function of the marine dinosaurs, the whales and dolphins, penguins, seals, walruses, and sea otters. In a broader sense, the four-limbed, backboned, five-digited conformation of the class of vertebrates may be a large general attractor, systematically distorted by the more local pull of species attractors.

There is absolutely no reason to suppose that such an iterative evolutionary attractor-seeking process might not be created within a cybernetic environment, one which would, moreover, operate at enormous speed, many orders of magnitude greater than that of ordinary biological evolution. A kind of pseudo-life would appear, perhaps based on a close analogy to the DNA molecule as its genetic archive, perhaps not.

Contemporary theoreticians of brain function—how brain generates and responds to mind—are now using a model of thought and memory which closely resembles the Darwinian process of natural selection, though like cybernetic processing it is blindingly faster. Many more new brain pathways are laid down, by neural growth and synaptic connections, than we could possibly use. Some patterns of connection are selected over others by their repeated correspondence with the sensory experience and pleasure-rewarded purposes of the individual, so that mental habits, skills, and memories are formed. It is known that the pleasure-chemicals of the brain—including those associated with the experience of beauty—are involved in laying down and reinforcing new synaptic pathways. Other possible patterns are pruned out—selected against. New experiences, and such continuous spontaneous reshuffling of connectivities as we experience in dreams, would produce a new range of variations upon which the selective process could work and whose survivors would be preserved in improved synaptic connections (dreams, then, playing for mental birth the role of sex in biological birth). Our enduring, and often pan-human symbols, ideas, myths and images might thus correspond to the strange attractors we have found elsewhere in nature.

If biological evolution can be copied in a cybernetic space, why not neural evolution? Artificial intelligence may not come into existence as a program we design, a set of instructions to a Turing Machine, but it may do so as the evolutionary result of a process we initiate; not as a calculation but as a reflexive entity carried and mediated by calculations.

But, after all, a male and female human being can, in the space of a few delightful minutes, create together an electrochemical organism which, with proper care and programming, will perform all those remarkable operations of reflection, imagination, and laughter to which we have referred. The real change, and the exciting prospect, arises out of the redefinition of the problem of AI, and the reconception of the arts, which is coming into being. Out of this reconception, in which art and AI are seen as two elements of the same process, a process which is also the creative dynamic of evolution and of nature in general, will come a cultural renaissance. If it does not happen here, then it will happen in Japan or Europe. No doubt there will be success in achieving the goal of AI, just as there has been success in creating artifical forms of life. But by that time, life and intelligence itself may be only two out of a range of kinds of transcendent self-organization previously unimagined.

The renaissances of fifth-century Greece, fifteenth- and sixteenth-century Europe, and of contemporary Japan similarly grew out of a whole reimagining of the relationships among art, science, technology, and the life of the spirit. We now have a new intellectual and imaginative goal, which might be called practical philosophy, or even practical theology: the creation, rather than just the analysis, of Mind. The arts and the sciences are both integral to this project, and will begin to lose their distinctness from one another in the process. The minds that we create, though we will share directly in them through various forms of cybernetic-neural communion, may surpass our unaided vision and moral goodness as would a god. They will be our miraculous children. We owe it to them, so to speak, to give them a good start in life.

# ANGELS FROM
# THE TIME
# TO COME

CERTAIN MOMENTS IN A GOOD story possess a quality that is logically very strange indeed, and which renders them haunting and unforgettable. Consider Dorothea's choice of Ladislaw as her lover in *Middlemarch*. The logic of fiction would dictate that Dorothea should pair up with Lydgate, who is a heavyweight like herself, and if after reading the first half of the book we were to try to predict the outcome, this would probably be our choice. On the other hand, when she upsets our expectations, we are on reflection not disappointed but deeply excited by the depth of what has happened. Strangely, we now realize that Dorothea's surprising choice was really inevitable all along, that it had to be that way; her originality, her tenderness, her St. Teresa-like sense of mastery could express itself no other way.

We get the same feeling when Edmund has his deathbed repentance in *King Lear,* and even more so when it turns out that his repentance, which would be the perfect deus ex machina to save Cordelia's life, ends up with no apparent plot function at all: in fact it makes Cordelia's death even more unexpected, arbitrary, and horrifying. Yet we recognize immediately the absolute rightness of this reversal; it was inevitable all along!

One could cite dozens of other examples: the *Odyssey* is a compendium of them, Faulkner is a master at the art, and so is Tolstoy. In music, the same thing happens. Mozart will often pile two or three twists of melodic or harmonic surprise upon each other, and yet, in retrospect, the structure of his piece will hold firm, perfectly braced, airy, yet as strong as adamant.

The peculiar thing about such moments is that, by their unpredictability before the event combined with their retrodictability after it, they radically defy the requirement that truth be independent of time; and yet they are by no means arbitrary or merely expedient—it is not as if the artist were irresponsibly flinging in extraneous incident or distorting the integrity of the work by arbitrary crowd-pleasing interventions. It was Plato who most clearly established the idea that truth cannot trim its sails with the winds of time, that two and two must equal four for all eternity, not just today, or on Wednesdays, or in the past but not in the future. Certainly there are kinds of coherent truth for which Plato's requirement of temporal indifference must hold. But he is perhaps wrong in implying that coherence and intelligibility—which are supreme virtues, or else we could not even reason about such matters, and must come to blows—are only possible under conditions of time invariance. Edmund and Dorothea and Odysseus and Quentin Compson and Anna Karenina are coherent and intelligible—so much so that a lifetime is not enough to appreciate how much. But much of what they do has the peculiar capacity to alter the past in such a way as to make certain futures inevitable, when they were not so before.

We need, then, a new logic to talk about such actions, one which always has two senses—a strong sense, which applies retroactively, and a weak sense, which applies prospectively. Recent developments in Italian philosophy have produced the expression "weak thought," which though it properly applies to the level of assertion and probability in a proposition, can well be used here as well. Researchers in cognitive science, the philosophy of mathematics, and artifical intelligence have all come to recognize that the work of the human mind cannot be modeled without some kind of soft linkage between concepts which relies on large vague databases, partial resemblances, and relative probabilities of truth. But what we want are laminated words, whose one face is weak and whose other is strong, and a reasonably rule-governed way of using them.

In the Oriental martial arts there is a fine practical vocabulary of concepts for dealing with such matters. A karate expert will view his or her opponent with "soft eyes," meaning that the attention is global rather than concentrated, and will achieve by this a decisive edge in speed over an opponent. But the martial arts vocabulary does not easily lend itself to philosophical speculation; and this essay is a kind of game or fiction in speculative philosophy. We can find in contemporary theoretical physics, perhaps, a more exactly defined set of terms: specifically, in John Archibald Wheeler's notion of the strong and weak anthropic principles. What this essay will do is explore some of the implications of the anthropic principle(s) for a subject, which, we will see, is in its essence bound up with time asymmetry: that is, the nature of angels.

A simple experiment will illustrate one of the most mysterious phenomena in quantum mechanics. Take two polaroid sunglass lenses and hold them against the light, one behind the other. If they are aligned so that their axes of polarization are parallel with each other, the two lenses together will let almost as much light through as one lens alone. But if you rotate one lens so that the axes of polarization are at an angle, the amount of light getting through will diminish until, when the lenses are at 90° to each other, no light gets through at all. A sunglass lens cannot bend the polarization of the light; all it can do is stop light which is vibrating in a north-south direction, say, and let light through that is vibrating in an east-west direction. Thus, it makes perfect sense that the two lenses should together stop all the light, since all the directions in which light could vibrate involve some combination of north-south and east-west.

The mystery appears if we place a third lens at about 45° between the two lenses that have already been set at 90° to each other. Commonsense would suggest that to do so would be superfluous because all the light has already been stopped, and total darkness cannot be further darkened. What actually happens, though, is this: *light now starts passing through the three lenses, when it could not pass through two!*

What does this mean? Quantum physics offers various explanations, all of which involve some deep and beautiful violation of common sense. One goes like this: a wave (or particle) of light before it reaches the lenses does not "know" what its polarization is, and the first lens forces the light to "make up its mind." However, it only has to make up its mind about one of the axes of polarization, not any others. If the second lens it hits absolutely excludes what the first lens absolutely permitted (90°) then all light is stopped. This is proved by the fact that if the 45° lens is placed on either side of the pair of opposite lenses, and not between them, it cannot alleviate the darkness, because the unmediated contradiction still exists. But if the middle lens is at 45° to the others, the light gets to make up its mind again, and by the time it reaches the third lens it has "forgotten" about the "decision" it was forced to make at the first lens; the light coming through the second lens is just light that has been through a northeast-southwest filter, and that is all it is. The third lens does not absolutely contradict the second, and thus about 1/4 of the original light gets through.

But something very peculiar has happened to the nature of time in this account. Events and objects are constituted by the information that they exchange with other events and objects and with themselves; and the means by which that information gets exchanged are, as forms of light, subject to quantum uncertainty. Which means that when the light that tells us of events in the filament of a light bulb, or on the surface of the sun, is forced to declare the orientation of its vibration, then the nature of the light bulb and of the sun becomes *retroactively* a little more definite. Reality is, when unobserved, only approximate in its nature: it is a probability function or "wave function" specifying a number of possible states which it might assume if challenged, at which time the packet of uncertainty that constitutes a particle before it is measured is "collapsed"—forced retroactively to make up its mind. Why "retroactively"? Because light, and any other form of information, is limited in the speed of its propagation, and anything we observe is already in the past of the observing eye.

Reality, then, depends partly on how we measure it. The two-lens system asks a different question of the world than the three-lens system, and thus the answer we get is different, and thus the reality of which we asked the question, and which is already in the past, must be different. Events do not occur in and of themselves, but exist in a kind of partnership with their observers. The "mighty world of eye and ear," as Wordsworth puts it, is made up of "what we half perceive, and half create."

Now this idea can be, and has often been, misinterpreted by those who—through wishful thinking, or malicious mischief against the noble and simple authority of science, or a preference for the moral excitement of our own opinion over what is demonstrable—desire to discredit the possibility of reasonably sure knowledge. Hence, the conclusion that some critics have drawn from a superficial study of quantum theory, that nature is incoherent, and dependent upon the ideological views of scientists, which in turn reflect the political system and its entrenched power and privilege, etc. And thus, such abominations as "Jewish science" in the thirties and "feminist science" now.

The fallacy lies in the fact that the "observing" and "measuring" that collapses the wave function can be performed by entities other than human beings. A rock can collapse a photon's wave function too, and the universe had a definite being, though a simpler and cruder one, before human beings evolved. Thus, the universe has been continually and cumulatively "making up its mind" through a consensus of exchange of information for fifteen billion years. We are now an increasingly important part of that consensus, but as Lysenko learned when his communist wheat died in Siberia, politics cannot resist a sufficiently negative vote by the inanimate public of the universe. By the time we observe most things that are larger than subatomic particles, they are already part of a healthy, functioning, mutually-supporting reality system, to be altered only if we know the fault lines of its construction and have the technology to pry them apart.

Let us revise our earlier formula about the partnership of events and their observers and say that events and objects, at least, need to be registered as such by some other event or object that has the selective sensitivity to do so. Many events and objects can be registered by very crude "observers," that need only be made of matter to do their job. Others, though—and here things get interesting—do need rather sophisticated observers; and there are many whose more complex aspects only come into existence at the call of such sophistication and sensitivity. Or, let us put it this way: the observer is enfolded, in whatever way the observer is capable, in the being of the prior event that is observed. If the observer is crude, its report will form part of the brute consensus of matter; but if the observer is very sensitive, new properties will appear, and will really begin retroactively to exist, within the past event that is observed. Organized forms of matter are more sensitive, have finer resonances, than amorphous ones; living things, animals and plants and so on, are more sensitive than stones; and we are more sensitive than animals and plants, if only because our sensitivity includes theirs (and if it did not, we could not even argue about their relative merits).

It was Wheeler's idea to apply this reasoning to the most important quantum event of all: the origin of the universe. In what sense was the origin of the universe a "quantum event"? The Big Bang theory, which best satisfies the evidence, requires that before it was $1/10^{20}$ second old the whole of the universe must have been packed into a space less than $1/10^{10}$ centimeters in radius, and this was all the space there was. It is precisely this realm of space and time within which quantum theory holds, and within which the role of the observer becomes important. We human beings are certainly the most obvious and sensitive observers of the origin—for instance, we are still picking up the background radiation of the Big Bang from all directions, a form of information about it that is direct and unmediated, if very old.

One of the greatest challenges to the cosmologist is why the universe originated with the precise numerical constants that it did. These constants include the inverse square law by which the force of gravitation diminishes with distance, the speed of light, the electron volt constant, Planck's constant, and so on. If these constants had been different in the slightest degree, no conceivable form of life could have evolved; indeed it is hard to see how even organized matter could have evolved. Why should we have had the astonishing luck to have got the exact origin that would bring about a universe which in the fullness of time would deliver us into existence?

Wheeler's anthropic principle answers this riddle elegantly by suggesting that of all the possible origin-states for the universe, only one would bring about observers of it that could collapse its wave function, ask it the question that would force it to declare a particular identity. Thus, the universe originated as it did, with that particular set of constants, because it was since seen to do so. Any other hypothetical universe would remain only an eternal possibility. We, its observers, necessitated an observer-producing origin; and our question about it, like Parsifal's, though long delayed, transforms the Waste Land of the original uncertainty into the rich and productive field of cosmic evolution.

However, this formulation of the idea is still a rather coarse one. There is, as we have already noted, a wide range of organisms between photons and human beings, of varying degrees of organization and complexity; from atoms which are sensitive to electromagnetic and gravitational information, through crystals, which are also sensitive to vibration, heat, pressure, and so on, to animals which can smell, see, and hear. All of these can act as observers and ask, in their own way, the fructifying question of Parsifal. Thus, it would be more accurate to say that as more and more sensitive observers evolved, they re-specified more and more exactly what the initial state of the universe must have been.

A later, more evolved and sophisticated organism collapses the wave function not only of the Big Bang but also of all prior organisms; either indirectly, through the Big Bang itself, or directly, because of its implicit observation of

quantum events within those simpler, earlier beings. Therefore, the chordates had to be as they were to bring about
vertebrate observers; vertebrates must be just so to occasion
mammalian observers, mammals to bring about primates,
and primates to be the ancestors of human beings. The fruit
of any process is also an observer of it and so a partial deter-
miner of its nature.

Wheeler's anthropic principle, thus generalized, now
seems to fit nicely our requirement for an intelligible account of time asymmetry. As we look forward toward a putative event, we need assume no more than the weak anthropic
principle: whatever that event, it will syllogistically bring
about a plausible future observer of it (or else there would
be no evidence that it had happened). As we look backwards,
we can assume the strong anthropic principle: that earlier
event was partly necessitated by the requirement that it
help produce a universe in which we can look back at it. And
the weak and strong principles are not isolated from each
other, but share a strange seam across their back sides, so to
speak, and form a kind of Janus, a sort of transitional January between the old year and the new. Through that semi-
permeable seam there is a leakage or tunneling of
implication or entailment, just as the present moment con-
ducts and mixes the different logical environments of past
and future into each other.

How strange this reasoning is! Indeed, before its logic
unfolded, it would have been utterly implausible to the mind
that now thinks it; and yet as each idea precipitates into
being, it opens up a new landscape in whose context a new
plausibility emerges. There must be something in it, so the
mind reflects, for the process itself is so like the very story
of real life!

For a new implication has just come over the horizon:
our own nature and activity, as well as being partly determined by past causes, and partly the result of the autono-

mous self-organizing iterative feedback of our own consciousness, must also be subtly guided and conditioned by
their own future observers. Our own wave function is being
collapsed by future awarenesses that we will help to bring
into being and which will in turn ratify our existence and
help us to fall into a definitive shape.

I know perfectly well that my own mind is not capable
in itself of those leaps or marvelous compactions into a new
thought which it undergoes in the process of composing a
poem or a creative essay. Perhaps this feeling itself, of there
being some niche or prepared receptor for the heavy current
of thought, some attractor that will emerge out of its turbu-
lence, was what the Greeks meant by the Muse. Sometimes
she speaks with unmistakable and imperious tongue (yet she
is so delicate, so easily deniable, is she not?), sometimes in
a still, small voice; but if one had never experienced her, and
suddenly heard her voice for the first time, one would be
convinced that one were in the presence of the supernatural,
or that one were hallucinating thoughts not of one's own
making. Only when she is, as she is, a daily source of insight
and surprised reminder, do we take her voice as normal and
unremarkable. But without it, how dull and dim the world
would be!

All cultures know of them, these spirits or kamis or
"presences/ That piety, passion or affection knows," as
Yeats put it, these beautiful and terrible animate forms that
visited Lot and Abraham and Jacob and Ezekiel. The report
of them is so widespread that they must represent some
reality. Let us name these future knowers of us, these ob-
server-participants in the creation and generation of our
nature and being. They are the angels.

But as the argument implies, they are not only the attractors and subtle guides of our action, our creative evolution. They are also its result. Angels are painted as babies,
as *putti;* of course, because they are our children, our unborn

descendants. Children—but evidently children winged with
incalculable power and complexity of purpose; as far beyond
us as we are beyond the dim wonderings of pithecanthropus;
as they were beyond the animals, plants, minerals, and physical particles that preceded them—those forerunners that,
by observing, we lend a more distinct being:

> Early successes, favorites of fond Creation,
> ranges, summits, dawn-red ridges
> of all forthbringing,—pollen of blossoming godhead,
> junctures of light, corridors, stairways, thrones,
> chambers of essence, shields of felicity, tumults
> of stormily-rapturous feeling, and suddenly, separate,
> mirrors, drawing up again their own
> outstreamed beauty into their own faces.

Rilke on angels, repeating much that we know from
Ezekiel and Blake and Giotto, and more strangely the ritual
art of Indonesia and China and Tibet, the dragon-forms of
Mayan vision-carvings, of African and Eskimo spirit-masks;
the authentic voice of the shaman.

If the angels are our children, what must we do to bring
them into being? For clearly they are so beautiful that we
ought to bring them into being. Having once experienced
them, one would be in no doubt of the value of one's own
existence, if one could have but the smallest role in opening
to them the gates of history.

We are at a remarkable juncture in our own history and
indeed of the history of the cosmos: when evolution becomes
fully self-aware, when nature finds the theme and mode it
has sought from the beginning. Not that the change that is
coming will be utterly unprecedented. We have always been
capable of directing our own evolution, in the traditional
way, by choosing mates who have the beauty and wit and
capacity for love and strength of mind that will lead the

species by increments toward the more deeply human; and we know the more deeply human as horse breeders know racing temperament and apple growers know a noble strain, even before we have good examples of what we are after. In like fashion, a poet recognizes the line or cadence or image as truly part of the unborn poem. But now that process has become irretrievably self-conscious, and is assisted by a more and more powerful battery of technical aids.

However shocking and terrifying is the idea of biological engineering, we cannot now lay it aside. If we want angels, should we not build and beget them? Genes can be altered, added, removed; and, more excitingly, new studies show that we use only a tiny fraction of our DNA, and that our development and mature being depends almost as much on a unique pattern of suppression and expression of the genes we already have, as on what the genes are to begin with. This pattern itself may be subject to craft and sculpture. Especially in this area, now known as epigenetics, and encompassing the older, more empirical sciences of embryology and development, some of the ancient enemies of humankind—cancer, aging, immune deficiencies, neurochemical diseases—now seem to be revealing their weaknesses.

Slowly, infinitely carefully, in fear and trembling, we will continue what we have already started—the correction of inherited diseases, the repair of genetic deficits, the tuning of the chemistry of mood, memory, and thought so as to express fully, rather than in its present muffled and crippled form, the special grandeur of each individual's inheritance. Those who are great artists, athletes, givers, scientists, lovers, know the sweet clarity and power of perfect work and action in moments that are tragically brief but which nevertheless make a lifetime worthwhile. But they also know the stifling burden of their own usual stupidity, forgetfulness, depression, irritated spite, and sheer incapacity: as when you look at a certain kind of problem in a field for which you have no talent, and nothing happens, the quick insight does not flow.

Why should not the whole human race be given the capacity to experience and use that intensely individual genius which we reverence in just a few? Let us not comfort ourselves in our present condition by false and vulgar prejudices: that genius is necessarily unhappy, that geniuses are all the same, that the greatly talented are necessarily unstable or lopsided in personality, that they lack the common touch, that they are impractical. These problems all people have, and, if anything, great genius is often remarkably free of them. The unhappiness of genius is less due to inherent flaws in the nature of genius itself than to the fact that having learned to fly, the genius feels more exasperatingly the crippling handicaps that all human beings labor under and the "inhuman dearth of noble natures" about them, as Keats put it. Perhaps, through biotechnical means, we may be able eventually to free the choked genius of our species, and having done this we would already be on the way to angelic intelligence and love. Of course, a caution is in order: the biotechnical tools will themselves take artistic genius of a high order to wield without oversimplifying the problems or their solutions.

But our future evolution may well proceed in a fashion which partially transcends the strictly biological altogether. Gradually, we are learning to approximate the capacities of the human mind by means of cybernetic artificial intelligence. Can there be any doubt that an understanding of the working of mind will follow our understanding of the working of life, and that just as we are now able to synthesize living matter, so we will be able to synthesize self-conscious thought and feeling and imagination? One day that evil distinction between the artificial and the natural will be thrown down, and we will have escaped the mind-forged manacles which alienate us from the creative and self-re-

flective evolution of the rest of nature. On that day we will
have extended our minds and spirit into dimension beyond
dimension; we will have a direct neural-cybernetic interface
with our thinking machines, and through them to all of
nature; we will feel as stones and flames and petals feel,
because the instruments by which we register their experience will be directly connected to our nervous systems. All
nature will be our home and our body.

And, of course, it always was, as the Zen sages tell us.
But it is a peculiar thing about us, that we can at best feel
only briefly and distantly the things that we know ought to
make this world, even at the worst of times, a very paradise
in every moment. We can know the infinitely interesting
miracle of being, but are most of the time somehow divided
as by a curtain from the actuality of it as experience. Why
should not nature be waiting for us, with our great natural
technical intelligence, to simply plug ourselves in to the
universe, to complete a new loop of feedback in the world?
Perhaps our unhappiness, our frustrated rage, our cruel de-
spair comes from the unconscious realization that though it
is what we were built for, we haven't got around to it yet.
Nature cannot do it by herself, and thus evolved us, a special
quintessence of the soul of nature, her "dearest-selved
spark," as Hopkins says, to do it for her. Perhaps the happiness of scientists and artists and saints is that they come
closest to this in-feeling and participation, though by means
which are only traditional and are as yet truncated, lacking
the new sensorium that needs to be added.

But the traditional means are certainly wonderful in
themselves. Indeed it will be a part of the new science to
recognize just how subtle and marvelous they are. The arts
are already an empirical craft of artificial intelligence, a
means of creating programs in paint, sound, stone, action, or
words that embody their makers' angelic insight yet survive
their makers to be reincarnated when booted into the brain

circuitry of other people. The traditional arts are also a way of getting access to the enormous integrating powers, the tact and instinct of nature at her best, that lie dormant in the human brain. Thus, they are an essential partner with the new science and technology in creating and begetting those future beings that we see in our visions of angels. By itself, the new technique would be shallow, a technical fix with possibly disastrous consequences: monsters or chilly abortions. Only when the sensibility of a Mozart, a Shakespeare, a Velazquez, a Murasaki, a Louis Armstrong is added to that of a Von Neumann or a Francis Crick, will the miracle have a chance of happening. And the artists themselves are special partly because they in turn have more immediate access to the angels they are helping to bring to birth. We can perhaps agree that if this work is not impossible, it might be a project as worthy as the building of the cathedrals and the construction of Classical Greek civilization—something to replace the anomie of our century with a commitment that the whole world can share.

There is a curious circularity in the last paragraph that will bring us to the last point in this exploratory essay. Let us digress for a moment. Recently brain science has been revolutionized by the new concept of "top-down" causality (Roger Sperry's term). Brain science still concedes that the components of the brain—its atoms, molecules, cells, and anatomy—indeed partially determine, in a "bottom-up" fashion, what happens on the holistic level of thoughts, decisions, feelings. But it is becoming increasingly clear that there exists a very powerful top-down causality, wherein we can change the chemistry and electrical activity of our brains by means of our choices, actions, knowledge, acquired habits, creative efforts, and willed attitudes: the whole governing the parts.

But if the lower hierarchical levels of the brain are both causing and being caused by the higher levels, then the

brain's activity is an essentially circular—or, better, a spiral
or helical—process. It is a feedback system determining itself and determining its own process of self-determining.
Now if the brain is an elegant microcosm of the universe—
and it would be hard to see how we could have survived as
a species if it were not, for otherwise it would always be
wrong about the world and thus have led us into extinction—
then the universe itself must be such a part-whole, top-
down/bottom-up feedback system too.

But it is also clear that the wholeness of the universe is
an emergent property. As more and more sensitive organisms evolve to observe it, escaping the relative solipsism of
the subatomic and atomic levels of being, so the universe
assumes more and more a coherent unity. On a starry night
we can see, in a sketchy and synoptic way, nearly half of it:
but it takes specially and recently evolved eyes and brains
to do so. If the holistic level of the universe is still only
emerging, then we must identify the past with part-to-whole,
bottom-up causality; and the future with whole-to-part, top-
down causality. That is, if the universe is something like a
brain, the brain-parts of the universe are its past, and its
mind is its future. We might even *define* the past and future,
and time itself, by means of such a distinction.

But if the process of determining, of causality, goes both
ways in time—bottom-up in the futurewards direction, top-
down in the pastwards direction—then the universe itself is
just such an iterative, spiral feedback system as is the brain.
It is not just a linear process, and we must abandon all
merely linear models of time. As a nonlinear system, the
universe is one of a class of systems now being investigated
by chaos theory, fractal mathematics, and the theory of nonlinear, dissipative, self-organizing dynamical processes.
Every event and object in the world has, in a sense, been
round and round the great circuit of material and final cause
an infinite number of times: its origins determining its pre-

sent state, its results determining its origins. Thus, every event in the world is infinitely rich; there is indeed infinity in a grain of sand, eternity in a flower. And this infinity, this eternity is not the vacuous and otiose thing that we find in classical metaphysics and set theory, but an active, open-ended, transformative infinity, a generativeness, like Chomskyan grammar. Every experience we have, if we were to see it properly, is infinitely deep, fully involving the creative and voluntary energy of the universe as a whole.

Here of course we are on the frontiers of theology: and before that prospect, the speculative tongue turns almost to stone. But there is one step between us and that blinding light, one further mediation or ratio of speculative understanding: the angels. And even if they do not exist, is not the very thought of them an active warrant of their reality as causes? For are not thoughts causes?

# FURTHER
# READING

ALEXANDER ARGYROS. *A Blessed Rage for Order.* Ann Arbor: University of Michigan Press, forthcoming.

MIKHAIL BAKHTIN. *The Dialogic Imagination.* Trans. Michael Holquist. Austin: University of Texas Press, 1981.

J.D. BARROW and F.J. TIPLER. *The Anthropic Cosmological Principle.* Oxford: Oxford University Press, 1986.

STEWART BRAND. *The Media Lab: Inventing the Future at M.I.T.* New York: Viking, 1987.

FERNAND BRAUDEL. *The Mediterranean and the Mediterranean World in the Age of Philip II* (3 vols.). Trans. Sian Reynolds. New York: Harper & Row, 1972.

EDWARD BRUNER and VICTOR W. TURNER, eds. *The Anthropology of Experience.* Chicago: Illinois University Press, 1986.

JOSEPH CAMPBELL. *The Hero With a Thousand Faces.* Princeton: Princeton University Press, 1949.

R.G. COLLINGWOOD. *The Idea of History.* Oxford: Oxford University Press, 1946.

DONALD COWAN. *Unbinding Prometheus: Education for the Coming Age.* Dallas: The Dallas Institute Publications, 1988.

ROBERT P. CREASE and CHARLES C. MANN. *The Second Creation: Makers of the Revolution in 20th-Century Physics.* New York: Macmillan, 1986.

E.G. D'AQUILI, C.D. LAUGHLIN, JR., and J. MCMANUS, eds. *The Spectrum of Ritual: A Biogenetic Structural Analysis.* New York: Columbia University Press, 1979.

PAUL DAVIES, *God and the New Physics.* New York: Simon & Schuster, 1983.

———. *The Cosmic Blueprint.* New York: Simon & Schuster, 1988.

SIR JOHN ECCLES, ROGER SPERRY, ILYA PRIGOGINE, BRIAN JOSEPHSON. *Nobel Prize Conversations.* Dallas, San Francisco, New York: Saybrook, 1985.

FREDERICK FEIRSTEIN, ed. *Expansive Poetry.* Santa Cruz: Story Line Press, 1989.

J.T. FRASER. "Out of Plato's Cave: The Natural History of Time." *Kenyon Review.* Winter, 1980.

———. *Time as Conflict.* Basel, Stuttgart: Birkhauser, 1978.

WILLIAM GIBSON. *Neuromancer.* New York: Ace, 1984.

———. *Count Zero.* New York: Arbor House, 1986.

JAMES GLEICK. *Chaos: Making a New Science.* New York: Viking, 1987.

ERVING GOFFMAN. *The Presentation of Self in Everyday Life.* New York: Doubleday, 1959.

———. *Interaction Ritual.* New York: Doubleday, 1967.

DAVID GRIFFIN, ed. *The Reenchantment of Science.* Albany: State University of New York Press, 1988.

———. *God and Religion in the Postmodern World.* Albany: State University of New York Press, 1989.

JAMES HANS. *The Play of the World.* Amherst: University of Massachusetts Press, 1981.

CHARLES HARTSHORNE. *Born to Sing: an Interpretation and World Survey of Bird Song.* Bloomington: Indiana University Press, 1973.

IHAB HASSAN. "The Question of Postmodernism," in Harry R. Garvey, ed., *Romanticism, Modernism, Postmodernism.* Lewisburg, Toronto, and London: Bucknell University Press, 1980.

———. *The Right Promethean Fire.* Urbana: University of Illinois Press, 1980.

———. *Selves at Risk.* Madison: University of Wisconsin Press, 1990.

STEPHEN W. HAWKING. *A Brief History of Time.* New York: Bantam, 1988.

DOUGLAS HOFSTADTER. *Gödel, Escher, Bach.* New York: Random House, 1979.

WILLIAM JAMES. *The Will to Believe, and other Essays in Popular Philosophy.* in *The Works of William James.* Cambridge, Mass.: Harvard University Press, 1979.

CHARLES JENCKS. *What is Post-Modernism?* London: St. Martin's Press, 1986.

WILLIAM JORDAN, ed. *Restoration and Management Notes.* Madison, Wisconsin. (periodical)

IMMANUEL KANT. *Kant's Critique of Esthetic Judgement.* Trans. J.C. Meredith. Oxford: Oxford University Press, 1911.

———. *Critique of Practical Reason.* Trans. L.W. Beck. Chicago: University of Chicago Press, 1949.

MELVIN KONNER. *The Tangled Wing: Biological Constraints on the Human Spirit.* New York: Harper & Row, 1982.

THOMAS KUHN. *The Structure of Scientific Revolutions.* Chicago: University of Chicago Press, 1962.

VLADIMIR LEFEBVRE. "The Fundamental Structures of Human Reflexion." *Journal of Social and Biological Structures,* 10. 1987.

KONRAD LORENZ. *On Aggression.* New York: Harcourt, Brace, and World, 1963.

JAMES LOVELOCK. *Gaia: a New Look at Life on Earth.* Oxford: Oxford University Press, 1979.

JAMES LOVELOCK and MICHAEL ALLABY. *The Greening of Mars.* New York: St. Martins Press, 1984.

JEAN-FRANCOIS LYOTARD. *The Postmodern Condition: A Report on Knowledge.* Trans. Geoff Bennington and Brian Massumi. Minneapolis: University of Minnesota Press, 1985.

BENOIT MANDELBROT. *The Fractal Geometry of Nature.* New York: Freeman, 1977.

LYNN MARGULIS and DORION SAGAN. *Microcosmos: Four Billion Years of Microbial Evolution.* New York: Summit, 1986.

DAVID MARR. *Vision.* New York: Freeman, 1982.

ROGER PENROSE. *The Emperor's New Mind: Concerning Computers, Minds, and the Laws of Physics.* Oxford: Oxford University Press, 1989.

ROBERT PIRSIG. *Zen and the Art of Motorcycle Maintenance.* New York: William Morrow, 1973.

DONALD POLKINGHORNE. *Narrative Knowing and the Human Sciences.* Albany: State University of New York Press, 1988.

ILYA PRIGOGINE and ISABELLE STENGERS. *Order out of Chaos: Man's New Dialogue with Nature.* Boulder, Colorado: New Science Library, 1984.

INGO RENTSCHLER, BARBARA HERZBERGER, DAVID EPSTEIN, eds. *Beauty and the Brain: Biological Aspects of Aesthetics.* Basel, Boston, Berlin: Birkhauser, 1988.

THOMAS J. SCHEFF. "Microlinguistics: A Theory of Social Action." *Sociological Theory,* 4, 1, 1968.

————. *Microsociology: Emotion, Discourse and Social Structure.* Chicago: University of Chicago Press, 1990.

J. WILLIAM SCHOPF, ed. *Earth's Earliest Biosphere: Its Origin and Evolution.* Princeton: Princeton University Press, 1983.

ERWIN SCHROEDINGER. *Science and Humanism: Physics in Our Time.* Cambridge: Cambridge University Press, 1951.

GEORGE A. SEIELSTADT. *At The Heart of the Web: The Inevitable Genesis of Intelligent Life.* New York: Harcourt Brace Jovanovich, 1989.

LYNDA SEXSON. *Ordinarily Sacred.* New York: Crossroad, 1982.

MARC SHELL. *The Economy of Literature.* Baltimore: Johns Hopkins University Press, 1978.

SORIN SONEA and MAURICE PANISSET. *A New Bacteriology.* Boston: Jones & Bartlett, 1983.

ROGER SPERRY. *Science and Moral Priority.* Oxford: Blackwell, 1983.

H.S. THAYER. "The Right to Believe: William James' Reinterpretation of the Function of Religious Belief." *Kenyon Review.* Winter, 1983.

HENRY DAVID THOREAU. *Walden.* 1854. Reprint. Columbus, Ohio: Charles E. Merrill, 1969.

FREDERICK TURNER. *A Double Shadow.* New York: Putnam, 1977.

————. *Natural Classicism.* New York: Paragon House, 1985.

————. *Genesis.* Dallas, San Francisco, New York: Saybrook Publishers, 1988.

————. *Rebirth of Value.* Albany: State University of New York Press, 1990.

VICTOR W. TURNER. *The Ritual Process.* Chicago: University of Chicago Press, 1969.

————. *Dramas, Fields, and Metaphors.* Ithaca: Cornell University Press, 1974.

————. *From Ritual to Theater.* New York: Performing Arts Journal Press, 1982.

JOHN VARLEY. *Demon.* New York: Berkley, 1984.

———. *The Persistence of Vision* New York: Dial Press, 1978.

JUDITH WECHSLER, ed. *On Aesthetics in Science*. Cambridge, Mass: M.I.T. Press, 1978.

HARVEY WHEELER, ed. *The Journal of Social and Biological Structures*. Carpinteria, California. (periodical)

JOHN ARCHIBALD WHEELER. "World as System Self-Synthesized by Quantum Networking." *IBM Journal of Research and Development*. January 1988, Vol. 32, No. 1.

ALFRED NORTH WHITEHEAD. *Science and the Modern World*. Cambridge: Cambridge University Press, 1967.

EDWARD O. WILSON. *Biophilia*. Cambridge, Mass.: Harvard University Press, 1984.

EDWARD O. WILSON and CHARLES J. LUMSDEN. *Promethean Fire*. Cambridge, Mass.: Harvard University Press, 1987.

GENE WISE. *American Historical Explanations*. Minneapolis: University of Minnesota Press, 1980.

LUDWIG WITTGENSTEIN. *Tractatus Logico-Philosophicus*. Trans. C.K. Ogden. New York: Kegan Paul, 1933.

VIRGINIA WOOLF. *A Room of One's Own*. Harcourt Brace & World, New York, 1929.

E.C. ZEEMAN. "Catastrophe Theory." *Scientific American*. April, 1976.